Quiet Moments

for moms

SCRIPTURES,

MEDITATIONS,

& PRAYERS

compiled by joyce williams

BEACON HILL PRESS
OF KANSAS CITY

Copyright 2008
By Joyce Williams and Beacon Hill Press of Kansas City

ISBN-13: 978-0-8341-2355-7
ISBN-10: 0-8341-2355-X

Printed in the
United States of America

Cover Design: Darlene Filley
Interior Design: Sharon Page

Library of Congress Cataloging-in-Publication Data

Quiet moments for moms : scriptures, meditations, and prayers / compiled by Joyce Williams.
    p. cm.
  ISBN 978-0-8341-2355-7 (pbk.)
  1. Mothers—Prayers and devotions. I. Williams, Joyce, 1944-

  BV4847.Q44 2008
  242'.6431—dc22

                                                        2007052807

10 9 8 7 6 5 4 3 2 1

CONTENTS

Susannah Wesley was once asked, "With all of your children, which one do you love the most?"

She replied, "I love the one most who is away from home until he returns, the one who is sick until he is well, the one who is hurt until the hurt disappears, and the one who is lost until he is found."

FOREWORD

Gracia Burnham

I'm a hands-on type mom. I have two kids left at home, and even though they're in their later years of high school, I'm at the school anytime I can be. I try to be very involved.

Several weeks ago I was decorating for the Music Department fundraiser. Every year we moms bake cheesecake and decorate so the kids can put on a musical show. A group of us were decorating in one area of the school while ball games and other activities were going on down the hall in the gym. We suddenly realized we were running low on decorations, so I volunteered to run to the store for more red and white streamers.

As I was walking across the parking lot and unlocking my car door, I heard a man in a truck nearby talking into his cell phone. No, he wasn't talking—he was yelling, something like "He made two points! Two [blankety-blank] points! If he's not going to apply himself and be aggressive and try a little bit, he may as well quit. I don't even know why I came today. He played a horrible game!"

My heart just wilted. Some guy was swearing about his son's performance—probably to his wife.

And then I thought—if we could go back 14 years with this same dad, I wonder if we might have heard him yelling, "Two steps! He took two steps! I was telling him to 'come to Daddy' and he did it!" He probably threw him up in the air and gave him a big hug. Who counted the times that little boy fell? Nobody. They just counted the times he succeeded.

When did this dad change from excitement when his kid tried to walk to nagging when he didn't perform perfectly? I thought, *I would never be like that! I would never treat my kids like that.* But as I drove to the store, I began thinking of all the times I nag the kids for not performing the way I want them to. How few times do I praise them for all the good things I see them doing? And I had to wonder when that happened for me. When did I change from encouraging them to do their best to being on their cases for not getting it just right?

Maybe I'm a bit more likely to see my own sin and short-comings since my jungle experience. Several years ago, my husband, Martin, and I were taken hostage by militant Muslims. We had left our three children with missionary coworkers at our home while we went to another island of the Philippines to work for a short time. We never returned home. After a year of captivity, Martin was killed. I was rescued and returned to the United States.

During that year, not a day went by that Martin and I didn't wonder about our children. We knew they had been sent back to the states and were receiving good care, but we missed them desperately. We wondered how they were doing emotionally. We prayed for them constantly and begged God to let us see them again.

I also relived all the times that I had been unkind to them, the times when I was impatient with them because they weren't *perfect*, the times when I was just plain mean! I prayed for the chance to do a better job of mothering. How thankful I've been that God has given me a second chance!

Probably the reason you picked up this book is that, like me, you want to be a better mom. You want to hear from others who have been there. I'm confident that we'll find encouragement, instruction, ideas, and maybe a few warnings that we need to hear as we read. May God work in all our hearts so that we'll become the mothers He wants us to be.

TRIBUTE TO MAMA

Joyce Williams

Many who are first will be last, and the last first.
—Mark 10:31

She was a very quiet, humble person. My mama avoided the spotlight like the plague, and you would never find her up front. As a matter of fact, she always sat near the back of the sanctuary.

Mama was unstintingly unselfish. She always made me and my sisters, Bobbi and Jane, her priority. I remember her taking us shopping. On rare occasions when Daddy had earned some extra money, she took us to one of the nicest stores in town. At great personal sacrifice she bought Jane and me, who were born 15 months apart, matching outfits. I don't remember her ever buying something for herself. That was Mama.

Mama and Daddy worked hard. It wasn't unusual for Daddy to work three jobs. Both of them had minimal educations, so survival was always a struggle. In the summer Daddy went to the farmers' market late in the day to buy bushels of produce. Mama spent many days canning fruits and vegetables to get us through the winter. For years she provided daycare for children in our home. We came to consider some of them as little "adopted" sisters and brothers.

In my early years Mama did our laundry each Monday—"wash day"—in a wringer washing machine. I remember being fascinated by the different galvanized tubs she positioned around that aging relic. One was for cold water, another for hot water, and another for bleach water. It was quite a process.

Jane and I took advantage of her preoccupation with that all-day assignment to stir up any kind of mischief we could. Mama believed in corporal punishment, so we frequently felt the sting of switches from nearby trees. From all I hear and remember, we must have been little terrors. One day she locked us in a room and told us not to "tear up jack," whatever that means. I was so ornery that I found a picture of Cousin Jack, and we tore it up! I wonder how child psychologists would analyze such behavior.

Mama was firm and really knew how to use a switch on two misbehaving little girls. But she was always kind and loving. She had a great sense of humor. I loved to hear her laugh, although she usually covered her mouth. She had lost several teeth, and due to her sacrificial nature, she delayed getting false teeth for years.

Although both of her parents were gone before I was born, Mama remained very close to her siblings. We loved visiting our aunts, uncles, and cousins. More than anything we enjoyed eating around a table groaning with delectable goodies! That was before we thought about sugar and fat, and we didn't count grams of anything. So everything was delicious and guilt-free.

One of my favorite memories of Mama was of her reading her big black Bible. Many times it would be opened to Revelation 21, because she loved to read about heaven. And she loved studying eschatology. Although she had to drop out of school after the sixth grade, she was highly intelligent and an avid learner.

I reflected about how the Lord comforted me the day Mama died. The call had come on a Sunday morning—Mama was gone. I was more than a thousand miles away, and my heart was broken. Gene and I could not get a plane out until Monday morning. I spent the afternoon and evening going through things of Mama's I had with me.

As I sorted through a box, I found an envelope I had never seen before. Her spidery handwriting brought fresh tears to my eyes. The words that I read through that misty veil lifted my heart.

Mama had always told us her favorite song was "Beulah Land," as sung by my daughter Bethany. So I was surprised to read, "My favorite songs are 'It Is Well with My Soul' and 'I'd Rather Have Jesus.'" My heart lifted as I thought, *What a great epitaph!* And I was comforted.

I was overwhelmed with sadness the week before our first Mother's Day without Mama. She was gone, and I was a thousand miles from both my daughters, Tami and Bethany. Word had just come that Uncle Lewis, the last of Mama's siblings and our patriarch, was dying of cancer. There was no way I could go to be with any of them. My heart was torn into ribbons of grief.

As I recalled the way the Lord had brought such wonderful words of comfort when Mama died, I was assured that somehow He would find a special way to console us once again as we walked back through the valley.

On Friday I called my cousin, Patsy. Tearfully, she said that Uncle Lewis' death was imminent. He almost died on Wednesday night but had somehow rallied. "As a matter of fact," she said, "he had been so much better the doctor sent us home to rest."

Early Thursday morning his nurse Debbie, a family friend, heard Uncle Lewis mumbling. She leaned toward him, listening. Joyfully, he whispered, "It's much more beautiful over there than I ever dreamed. Look at the angels! There's a big river. I can see lots of people on the other side." He paused, then said, "I see Mary!" Then he drifted back into unconsciousness.

After Patsy told me that story, I couldn't speak for the tears flowing down my cheeks. He had seen his sister Mary—Mama! Uncle Lewis had been given a glimpse of heaven and that very special resident. Joy infused me, pushing back the sorrow! What a Mother's Day gift—straight from heaven!

Patsy called early Saturday morning to tell me that Uncle Lewis had joined Mama. Rather than the sorrow I had anticipated, I was suffused with comfort as I pictured Mama welcoming him. I visualized brother and sister exploring heaven together. I could picture them walking with their new bodies on golden streets hand-in-hand, shouting joyfully. I'm sure Daddy was holding Mama's other hand as they helped to reacquaint Uncle Lewis with so many who had gone ahead.

Imagine! My humble, meek, back-of-the-crowd mother was right up front, by the portals of heaven! That Mother's Day was a joyous celebration rather than a sad farewell.

Prayer: *Thank you, Father, for allowing my meek mother to be a heavenly greeter.*

Thought for the Day: When our lives are over and we want to leave a final testimony as a legacy of our faith, the songs "I'd Rather Have Jesus" and "It Is Well with My Soul" say it all.

2

PRECIOUS MEMORIES

Judy Horn Anderson

Praise be to the God and Father of our Lord Jesus Christ,
the Father of compassion and the God of all comfort.
—2 Cor. 1:3

It seemed like just another ordinary evening. I had no way of knowing I would never forget that night in August 2001.

My husband, Daryl, and I were still sitting at the table after dinner at the home of Marvin and Ellie Martin. Marvin said, "How 'bout let's just go around the group and share a favorite childhood memory? It'll be a great way to get to know each other better."

We were enjoying another evening of sharing together in what we call "tables of eight." It's an excellent way to get to know three other couples from our large Encouragers Sunday School Class. That's exactly what we want to do—affirm and uplift each other. So we took turns journeying back into our yesterdays.

Some reflected on travels, others on family gatherings and holidays. When it was Marvin's turn, he began telling about a special Colorado vacation his family had taken when he was a teenager. He said, "We went to Evergreen—some kind of dude ranch."

As he continued, he painted an enchanting word picture so poignantly that we could almost smell the pine trees and see the snowcapped top of Long's Peak. Horse lover and fisherperson that I am, I felt I could just about nuzzle my face into the soft noses of the saddle horses and then pull in a huge fish from the stream in front of the big lodge. It almost seemed that I was walking in Marvin's memory with him.

Then he went on to say, "I remember this man and lady who operated the big lodge. She was very pretty and had a beautiful voice. She even sang every evening at suppertime!"

By that time my pulse was beating rapidly as I asked, "Marvin, what year did your family take that trip?"

He said, "Oh, let's see. I would have been about 15 years old, so it would have been the summer of '35 or '36."

I think he was a little surprised at my strong interest, especially when in my excitement I asked, "Where was the big lodge in relation to Evergreen?"

He thought about it for a moment and said, "We drove around the city lake and up a really gorgeous canyon."

No longer able to contain myself, I squealed, "Marvin! That lady with the beautiful voice was my mother! And that lodge was called Bendemeer Lodge! And that gorgeous canyon is called Upper Bear Creek Canyon!"

I went on to tell him that there's even a song called "Bendemeer's Stream" that's named after a brook in Ireland. My excitement swelled as I told him I still have an old yellowed copy of the sheet music. As a matter of fact, I had previously shared that with Marvin's daughter Linda, who is an accomplished vocalist.

All of us around the table sat there with our mouths hanging open. Who could believe that a random evening of food, fun, and reminiscing could result in such shared memories?

I could hardly wait to tell my aged mother. She was quite ill in August 2001, but her mind was still sharp. To this day I cherish the memory of sharing Marvin's story about Bendemeer Lodge and especially what her singing had meant to him. It was particularly significant because she passed away in December of that year.

Mother's Day 2002 was a sad day for me because it was my first Mother's Day without my own mother. Some 44 years earlier, my father had died suddenly from a massive heart attack. As an only child, I was now experiencing the painful and conspicuous loss of both my parents.

I wiped away a few tears as we drove to church that Mother's Day morning. We had just sat down when Marvin came into our Encourager's Class carrying a black-and-white photo of him sitting on a horse. The snapshot had been taken beneath a large entrance sign that hung across the road leading to the big lodge. Across the top of the entrance sign in that perfectly preserved photo were the words "Bendemeer Lodge." What a kind act of comfort and encouragement that picture was to me!

As I clutched that old photo to my heart, I thought, *How*

like our Father to reserve such a precious memento to comfort me in my grief! Could He have sent an angel to deliver that precious photo on such a heartrending day? With tears of joy and comfort flowing, I felt that on that special day a part of Mother was still with me.

Prayer: *Thank you, Lord, for precious memories.*

Thought for the Day: "The God of all comfort ... comforts us in all our troubles (2 Cor. 1:3-4).

3 ALWAYS FAITHFUL

Karen Anderson

Without faith it is impossible to please God, because anyone who comes to Him must believe that He exists and that he rewards those who earnestly seek him.
—Heb. 11:6

It was a warm Sunday evening in Minnesota. I usually would have been enjoying conversing with my Christian friends, but this night I was deep in thought, lost in another world.

My husband, Mark, and I had recently made a decision that would drastically change our lives. We were leaving the safe, secure world of a weekly paycheck to join Youth with a Mission (YWAM), which required a new kind of faith. YWAM is an interdenominational and international missions agency whose staff raise their personal support.

There was a battle going on in my mind; the enemy was whispering that we wouldn't be able to make it. Again and again I kept wondering how we were going to support our four children. (Two more children were later added to our family.) My mothering heart was anxious as flashes of bills to be paid ran through my head. Thoughts of mortgage payments, future college expenses, and all the other cares of this life tempted me to fall into fear and worry. Asking people to partner with us financially was a humbling task that challenged my Scandinavian mindset of "We can take care of ourselves."

I entered the church Mark had pastored for 10 years for the evening service. It was an intercity church in a troubled neighborhood. The people there were genuine, not afraid to be who they really were. We had the most interesting mix of people. Single moms, businessmen, those struggling with sexual identity, home schooling families, and others dealing with many types of issues and challenges were represented in our congregation.

Sunday evening services were my favorite. The crowd was smaller, yet those who came seemed to be the people who really wanted to be there. As a result, there was often a warm sense of the Lord's presence. That evening I really needed to hear from God to calm the fear and anxiety raging inside me.

The atmosphere was so sweet. I abandoned myself in worship, feeling spiritually needy for a touch from Him. I had to know that we were on the right path joining YWAM, that walking away from a weekly paycheck and depending on Him was not being irresponsible. I also wondered how our kids would fare. It takes a lot of money to care for a family of six, and I knew the needs would increase as our children grew older.

Mark was speaking that night, and at the end of the message he gave an altar call for those who wanted prayer and needed a touch from God. I was one of the first to respond. I was feeling desperate to know His peace. I knelt down at the front of the sanctuary.

Lord, I really need to know that this is the right thing we're doing, I prayed. *Help me, Lord.*

As always, the Lord answers the hungry, searching heart.

The response that came to me was *Do your children wonder where they will get their food every morning when they get out of bed?*

I answered the question in my heart, *No, Lord—they wake up every morning knowing that they'll be fed and their needs will be met.*

If you as a mother take good care of your children, how much more will I take care of mine? was the response that came to me.

A flood of love and peace swept over me. It was as if God was speaking to me as a Father would tenderly talk to his daughter. I immediately felt assured that His love was far more powerful than the fears I had allowed to come into my heart and that our Heavenly Father would provide for our family's needs. From that point on, I knew we were in God's will and that everything would be fine.

That was a turning point in my faith walk. I not only was confident in the Word of God that my needs would be met, but I also felt His assurance in a personal way.

Finally, I knew I was ready for the next adventure in our lives. That was 15 years ago, and the Lord has never failed us in our walk with Him. He has provided for us through many different means. We have learned to live by faith. In turn, He has always been faithful. Our family has truly been kept by the faith that we have kept.

Prayer: *Heavenly Father, may your perfect peace guard my mind and thoughts in your truth.*

Thought for the Day: The faith walk is an ever-growing experience—a walk that will not be totally realized until the day we see our Lord face-to-face.

THE PRAYERS OF TWO GRANDMOTHERS

4

Susan Meredith Beyer

Again, I tell you that if two of you on earth agree about anything
you ask for, it will be done for you by my Father in heaven.
For where two or three come together in my name,
there am I with them.
—Matt. 18:19-20

I must have shared a thousand stories with other grand-parents since I joyfully joined these wonderful ranks of the ob-noxious. All of us agree that there is nothing on earth more special than having our own perfect grandchildren.

We're compelled to show pictures at the slightest provo-cation. Somehow, we're oblivious to the patient smiles of those who are kind enough to listen one more time to our ravings about them.

It makes us wonder why we couldn't have had our grand-children first. We're a bit wiser, more attentive, and much bet-ter at parenting by the time grandchildren arrive. To be honest, sometimes we're a bit anxious about these precious little peo-ple. After all, we raised their parents.

We love these little extensions of ourselves, and we look forward to being with them for any reason or for no reason at all. And one of the perks is that we can send them home to their parents when they're not being so wonderful. But each new step, each new word, and the wonder in their eyes as we read their favorite stories for the tenth time are fresh blessings. Hearing their most curious questions, the magic that kisses away boo-boos, and knowing we're loved by them in a way that makes us feel that we are also somehow perfect is priceless.

I remember when my daughter Mindy and her husband, Tim, told me they were expecting their first child—my second grandchild. I was overjoyed!

I thought I detected the faintest hint of reservation in Mindy's voice, but I didn't question her at the time, remembering how exciting and scary pregnancy can be. Hormones go wild, causing us to weep for no reason and throw up at the mere suggestion of what were once favorite foods. We crave delicacies that threaten to magnify our figures way beyond baby-weight as we're bombarded with well-meaning but frightening life-as-you-know-it-is-about-to-change-forever comments.

Only the reassurance of more experienced women keeps us from spinning off into the air like a deflating balloon. The next several months bring times of learning, growing together, discovery, panic, swollen ankles, indescribable pain, and eventual joy. That cycle will actually repeat itself until our baby is—oh, about 40!

One day when I was visiting Mindy she asked, "What if I

can't really love my baby, Mom?" The question had apparently been on her mind for some time, and she was finally saying it out loud. I don't remember my response being terribly profound then, but I was concerned about her fears. I remember saying, "Don't worry, Mindy—you'll love your baby!" praying it would be true.

Finally the call came: Mindy was in labor. When I got to the hospital I was amazed at her high-tech birthing room. My experience two decades earlier had been much different.

I remembered the day Mindy was born. Hard labor came on so fast that her father and I barely made it to the hospital before her birth. She was perfect! Years before, her older brothers, Mike and Kevin, had also been in the same apparent hurry to be born. The doctor had suggested that with my third pregnancy I might consider living at the hospital for the final two weeks before my due date.

Although the monitor next to Mindy's bed seemed to be having the actual labor pains, she was pretty calm. I remembered her previous question and wondered if her calm spirit was a sign that she had made peace with the answer or if she was somehow steeling herself against caring in case anything went wrong. I prayed silently as Tim's mom (Granny) and I waited.

It wasn't long before Mindy seemed to have some really intense pain. Only Tim was allowed in her room. Granny and I waited in the hallway, listening for that precious first cry.

We began to sense something was wrong. Suddenly the door opened, and the nurse ran out. We could see the doctor holding a tiny infant, purple as an eggplant and looking like a pillow banded tightly in the middle.

"Oh, no—please, God, no," the doctor pleaded as he tried to wedge his finger under the umbilical cord that was obviously strangling the baby. We were on our feet now, watching everything that was happening as the doctor tried to revive our lifeless grandson.

In one unexpected move, Granny and I slammed into an embrace just like two giant hands had thrown us together. We prayed as if with one voice for the life of little Ryan. Finally, we heard a small, hesitant cry, then a full-blown scream—music to our ears. "Thank you, Lord, for this perfect grandson," we cried over and over.

Mindy need not have worried about being a caring mother. She was perfect and loving. I've learned much about how to be a mother, as I've watched my daughter.

Now all these years later I am so very thankful to have been blessed with the miracle of my children, grandchildren, and now great-grandchildren. All of them continue to teach me things I need to know.

At Ryan's high school graduation in 2006, I reflected on the day he was born 18 years earlier. In cap and gown, our Ryan—a handsome, totally healthy young man—represented God's loving answer to the most fervent prayer of two grandmothers.

Although Granny has now gone to heaven, somehow I believe she knew about Ryan's special day and was smiling at our shared answer to prayer.

Prayer: *Father, may my children seek first the only answer that will make the difference in their own lives, your Son, Jesus Christ.*

Thought for the Day: The best thing we can do for our children and grandchildren is to stay on our knees.

5 OBEDIENCE IN THE SMALL THINGS

Donna Bond

*Hear, O Israel, and be careful to obey so that it may go well with
you and that you may increase greatly in a land flowing with milk
and honey, just as the LORD, the God of your fathers, promised you.*
—Deut. 6:3

Our middle son, David, struggled with ear infections. By the
time he was two he had already been hospitalized twice, staying five days each visit. He had three sets of tubes put into his
ears as well as having his tonsils and adenoids removed.

David was scheduled for ear surgery because his eardrum
had collapsed for the third time, and we were once again at
the office of his ear, nose, and throat specialist for the pre-op
appointment. His eardrum had grown to the bones in his in-
ner ear. The surgery would cause some hearing loss, but it
would prevent deafness in that ear.

The week before that appointment, we had been praying
for David. The Lord told Jim to take David to his men's Bible
study on Tuesday morning to ask the men to lay hands on
David and pray for him. Jim felt the Lord had told him He was
going to heal David and bless him with musical abilities.

Jim got up early Tuesday morning and made the 15-minute drive into town to Bible study alone. As the men were eating breakfast, he felt the Lord tap him on the shoulder and say, *Jim, I told you to bring David to the Bible study.* He left his breakfast there and told the guys that he had something to do and that he would be right back.

He drove back to our house. We were all still asleep. He picked David up—Superman pajamas, blankey, and all—and carried him out to the car. He drove back into town and carried David into the restaurant where the men met for Bible study and prayer in a little room at the back.

Jim explained what God had told him to do. The men laid hands on David and prayed specifically for his healing. Then Jim brought David home and explained everything to me.

I reflected back to that morning as David sat on my lap as the doctor examined him. Jim and I watched as he looked in David's left ear. With a puzzled expression, the doctor looked in his right ear, then his left again.

"Now, which ear had the problem?" We smiled. We knew that his left ear had been healed. We told the doctor we had been praying for David. We told him about Jim's men's Bible study and how they had prayed. We rejoiced and celebrated.

David is now 18 years old and has led the teen praise band at our church. This year at teen camp, he was approached by a public relations director of a Christian university asking him to sing in one of their groups. We rejoice that David is gifted with many talents, and as God promised, music is among them.

We've been able to share this story many times. We believe God is able to heal! This is one of our Bond family faith-building stories, a lesson in faith as well as obedience. We talk to our children about it. What if Dad had not obeyed the Lord? What if he had not gone back to get David? What blessings would we have missed?

I know God wants to heal us and help us in troubled times, but I also know that God is more interested in our character than our comfort. Maybe obedience rather than healing was the key issue here. What do you think?

Prayer: *Father, thank you for hearing me when I pray. Help me to be radically obedient to you.*

Thought for the Day: The test of a man's religious life and character is not what he does in the exceptional moments of life but what he does in the ordinary times. (Oswald Chambers)

THE ARK OF GOD'S CARE

Rhea Briscoe

"If you can do anything, take pity on us and help us."
"'If you can'?" said Jesus. "Everything is possible for him who
believes." Immediately the boy's father exclaimed, "I do believe;
help me overcome my unbelief!"
—Mark 9:22-24

As the mother of seven children, I've often cried out to God like this father who brought his son to Jesus. Facing a crisis in his son's life, the father approached Jesus in expectation that He would help. In the shadow of the son's deep need and this father's now-evident lack of faith, he honestly and humbly replied, "I do believe; help me overcome my unbelief!" Frankly, I relate to that response.

As my husband, Dave, and I endeavor to raise our children in the fear and admonition of the Lord, I'm fully aware that although I believe wholeheartedly in the power of God and in His endless ability, when it comes to my children I often struggle with areas of unbelief. During those times, like the father in Mark's gospel, the cry of my heart is "I do believe; help me overcome my unbelief!"

Can you relate? Do you really believe that God has your children's best interest at heart? When they're faced with difficulties and tribulations, are you able to rest in the confidence that He loves your children more than you do? Are you convinced that whatever happens, God is completely and utterly in control and will use whatever situation your children face for their benefit and for His Glory? *O Lord, we want to believe! Help our unbelief.*

My son Tyler is a senior at Bethel University in St. Paul, Minnesota. Several weeks ago I received a frantic telephone call from one of his friends. She was calling from an ambulance that was in the process of transporting Tyler to the hospital. Apparently he had been knocked unconscious during a college rugby game and had suffered a severe concussion.

As she spoke, panic overtook me, and fear rose in my heart. She was calling from Minnesota, and I was six hours away in Wisconsin. What would I do? Who would take care of him? What if he needed me? Quietly, I heard the voice of the Father softly reassuring me that He neither slumbers nor sleeps and was actively on the job. "Be still, and know that I am God" (Ps. 46:10, KJV) echoed in my head. How could I be still when I was unsure of what was happening to my son hundreds of miles away?

I was suddenly overwhelmed with the realization that no matter how much I wanted to, I was not able to protect my son or keep him from danger. I had no choice but to let go and trust God. Why did I struggle with trusting the One who formed that child in my womb to do what was best for him? "I do believe," I cried. "Help my unbelief, Lord."

As I prayed for Tyler that day, I reflected on the faith of Moses' mother, Jochebed. Like me, when realizing she could no longer protect her child from impending danger, she came to a place of surrender.

Pharaoh, King of Egypt, had issued an edict requiring that all Hebrew male children be put to death. Jochebed knew Moses was in grave danger, so she hid him in an ark sealed with pitch and then placed him in the reeds along the bank of the Nile. The Bible tells us she did this because she realized *she was no longer able to hide and protect him from danger.*

What a powerful word for mothers today! As much as we would like, we are not able to hide and protect our children from danger—only God has that ability. All we can do is place them in the ark of God's protection and seal them in with our prayers and intercession.

Knowing that the Nile River was home to many kinds of venomous snakes, crocodiles, and other dangerous animals, I marvel at Jochebed's faith. These threats, as well as diseases and temperature changes, would have been a constant threat to infant Moses. Like me, Jochebed came to a place of surrender, a place of letting go, believing that the One in whom she trusted was far more powerful than the danger surrounding her child. She did what she could and then trusted God with the rest. He was faithful.

We must learn to release our children into the hands of One bigger than our situation, bigger than the storms of life, and bigger than the problems our children will confront. He will be their Strong Tower, Jehovah Jireh, the Lord their

Provider, and most important, the God who will *always* be there. As parents who have nestled their children in the ark of God's care, we can rest in knowing He will be their great I Am and will be everything they have need of when they need Him to be everything He is.

By the way, just in case you were wondering, Tyler recovered nicely from his traumatic ordeal—amazingly without the help of his overprotective mother!

Prayer: *Father, help me learn to simply say, "Lord, I do believe."*

Thought for the Day: God does His deepest work in you when you are in the deepest distress. You see, He loves you too much to let you miss His best. (Author Unknown)

7

THE NIGHT SEASON

Joyce Williams

[He] gives us songs in the night.
—Job 35:10

"I'm afraid you've had a heart attack." Those scary words spoken by a cardiologist in April 2006 certainly grabbed my attention—making me feel as though I were about to have a heart attack!

I leaned forward in my chair and listened intently to his grim statements. "Your stress test showed numerous abnormalities. We must schedule a heart catheterization right away."

It was a frightening time. As a wife, mother, grandmother, and great-grandmother—I had a lot of living I still wanted to do!

A few days later I lay on the cold steel table in an antiseptic operating suite watching the probing catheter snaking up into my artery. Suddenly everything shifted into high gear. The doctor yelled, "We need nitro! Get some Plavix!" The nurses scurried around, pumping pills down my throat and placing a tablet under my tongue.

When I was stabilized, the doctor leaned close and said, "The good news is that you've not had a heart attack, but the bad news is that you have multiple arterial blockages. We can schedule open-heart surgery, or you can opt for stents. What do you think?"

Truly, I wasn't thinking very clearly. It was obvious we were in the middle of a crisis. So I responded, "You're the doctor. What do you recommend?"

He recommended the stent procedures, so I weakly agreed to that. He proceeded with placing two stents right then. Afterward I asked him if we were done.

"No," he said. "You'll need to come back for several more stent placements. In addition to these blockages, the arteries to both kidneys show significant constrictions as well." Those were not words I wanted to hear. Suddenly I was face-to-face with my mortality.

It had happened so quickly. At almost 62, I was not *that* old. In a routine pre-op exam before having outpatient knee surgery, I just happened to mention I had been experiencing some chest discomfort. The surgeon ordered an EKG. The cardiologist didn't like what that test showed, so he ordered a stress test. He *really* didn't like that! Thus, the heart cath was scheduled.

It was twilight when they rolled me into a room in the coronary care unit. As the final rays of daylight faded from my tiny window, I realized that I had been transported into a night season of my life. Lying perfectly still for six hours as the night marched on, I reflected on the grim realities I had encountered.

Frankly, I was frightened. Coronary disease was prevalent in my family. My daddy had died at 59 from a second heart attack. Genetics were not good on either side of my family. When I was 30, my family doctor instructed me to lose at least 10 pounds, start walking, get on meds for hypertension, eliminate caffeine and salt from my diet, and so on. I did all those things and thought I was OK. After all, I eat oatmeal for breakfast! When Gene and I were married, I told him about my family history. Then I added, "*You're* my best 'Gene'!"

As the clock slowly ticked away those dark, lonely, night hours, I prayed and talked to my Father—the Great Physician. There was so much I still wanted to do. Gene and I have a very active speaking and writing ministry.

Upon Gene's retirement after 47 years of pastoral ministry, God led us to found and direct Shepherds' Fold Ministries. Our primary mission is to encourage and uplift pastors and their families. In the past eight years we have been blessed to travel more than 750,000 miles, crisscrossing the United States as well as ministering in more than 20 other countries. Gene says that if this is retirement, we're going to get jobs!

I dozed a little but jolted awake again around 3:00 A.M. when the nurse came in to remove the catheter from my groin. It was such a relief to be able to move again. She had discovered that I was in ministry and wanted to talk about the Lord. It was a joy to pray with her.

After she left 45 minutes later, the words to an old hymn began flooding my thoughts—especially the phrase about "in the night season" I racked my brain trying to remember the rest of the words and the title. Something about "shady green pastures, some through the fire." Then I remembered the title: "God Leads Us Along."

On a recent assignment with the Billy Graham team, when Gene and I were teaching for the Schools of Evangelism at The Cove near Asheville, North Carolina, we had listened as dear Bev Shea sang those wonderful words. Although I was in a desperate night season, my Father was holding me—leading me along!

In those predawn hours in a darkened hospital room, I began to feel that familiar heart tickle of the overshadowing presence of my Heavenly Father. None of the machinery to which I was attached reflected that moment, but tears of joy and peace began to flood over me. Those precious words washed away my fears and anxieties, and I softly sang along:

In shady green pastures, so rich and so sweet,
God leads His dear children along.
Where the water's cool flow bathes the weary one's feet,
God leads His dear children along.

Sometimes on the mount where the sun shines so bright,
God leads His dear children along.
Sometimes in the valley in darkest of night,
God leads His dear children along.

Some through the waters, some through the flood,
Some through the fire, but all through the blood.

Some through great sorrow, but God gives a song
In the night season and all the day long.

—G. A. Young

Although my cardiologist may not have approved, it seemed as though my heart swelled with joy and reassurance.

The next Sunday morning as Gene and I sat in a worship service, I began to weep when the praise leader began to sing, "In shady green pastures so rich and so sweet, God leads His dear children along . . ."

Once again, as I bowed my head, I felt that overwhelming assurance. Although I was still in the "night season," He had given me a song! Our Father, who specializes in working the night shift, would lead me. And peace flooded my soul.

Prayer: *Thank you, Father, that you never slumber or sleep.*

Thought for the Day: The light of the *Son* can penetrate life's darkest nights.

8 JUST BECAUSE I ASKED

Gail Buchanan

You do not have because you do not ask God.
—James 4:2

Easter week is always a special time for me to stop and once again reflect on Christ's passion as He demonstrated unconditional love for all humanity. As a mother, wife, and Christian, I want to fully experience this love and truly manifest the power of His resurrection in my life. I had been reading James 4, so I finally began asking for that resurrection power on Easter Sunday 2007.

Our church choir had been preparing for "Living Pictures of Easter," a huge, awesome but exhausting presentation reliving Jesus' last days. After many practices and several performances, our voices were very tired.

In 1982 I underwent a laryngoscopy to remove nodules from my vocal chords that had resulted from three years of elementary vocal music teaching. My career as a music teacher ended abruptly. It took nearly five years of vocal rest and going to many specialists before I could sing again.

Throughout those years, fatigue, stress, or a simple cold would trigger laryngitis or frustrating hoarseness. That's where I found myself on that Easter Sunday morning. It was debilitating not being able to sing. Although our son Matt was graduating from college, Emily is still in high school. I really needed my voice for many reasons. During this very trying time, my husband, Tim, was very supportive and encouraging.

That afternoon I tried to sing a little to prepare for the presentation that evening. My voice just kept cutting out. As Emily and I climbed into the car to head to church, I popped the CD soundtrack into the car's player, trying to sing through my solo. I could barely make a sound.

Anxiously, Emily asked, "Mom, what are you going to do?"

I whispered, "I don't know, but I'm afraid they're going to have to find someone else to sing for me."

The choir gathered to share communion before the presentation. Shawn, our minister of music, encouraged us to give God everything—not to withhold anything—just as Jesus had so willingly offered up the incredible sacrifice of His life. As the elements were distributed, each of us prayed quietly.

I bowed my head and told the Lord, *Right now, I don't have much to offer. My voice is nearly gone. I'm so tired and weary. O Lord, you have my heart, soul, and body. Please touch my vocal chords.* Then I picked up the cup. As I drank, I prayed, *Father, please heal the swelling right now.*

As the liquid poured down my throat, He reminded me that His blood had been spilled. The same blood that covers all our sins can also heal our bodies. He continued to whisper in my heart, *I did all this for you.*

And I tearfully replied, *Yes, Lord, you did, and I am so thankful.*

Immediately after I whispered those words, the aching in my throat left me, and I said, *OK, Lord—I trust you completely for what you have just done for me.* As I stood with the choir to sing the first three songs, I was hesitant to try to use my full voice. But as I began singing, a very warm spiritual blanket seemed to be wrapped around my shoulders, embracing me. It was like a strong, tender hug. I knew Jesus was holding me.

I could hardly sing for tears streaming down my face as I prayed, *O Lord, thank you. I feel the strength of your embrace. Please don't let go until I sing my solo. I know I can't do this in my own strength.*

As I stepped to the microphone I felt Him release me. He sang through me that night in an amazing way. Afterward, I could talk in my normal, strong, clear voice.

Emily rushed to me and said, "Mom, what happened? I was so surprised you were able to sing! You've never sung better!"

I tearfully replied, "Oh, Emily—the Lord healed my voice during communion."

My friend Donna came up to me afterward and asked what had happened on stage that night, because something seemed different. Then she said, "You sang as never before."

Joyfully I replied, "I gave Jesus everything—even my tired, weary throat, and He healed me!"

Since that resurrection evening, I've been singing a different song—just because I finally asked.

Prayer: *Thank you, Father, for hearing my faintest whisper.*

Thought for the Day: "Ask and it will be given to you; seek and you will find; knock and the door will be opened to you. For everyone who asks receives" (Matt. 7:7-8).

9

MOTHER-IN-LOVE

Judie Eby and Angela Eby

He answered their prayers because they cried out to Him.
—I Chron. 5:20

The fallen nature of our world defines the relationship between a mother and daughter-in-law as distasteful at best. In the book of Ruth, however, we find the relationship between Ruth and Naomi to be a beautiful thing. Even after the man that connected them was gone, they chose to continue caring for one another's needs. *Law* dictated they were bound no longer to one another; *love* compelled them to stay the course.

Judie, before she became a mother-in-law, lost her brother to war. She came from a family that attended church, but her faith was nominal at best. She had been somewhat of a wild child, involved with friends who committed petty theft and were generally mischievous. Her mother, though, prayed and led by quiet example. Looking back now, she can see how her mother's love and care kept her from serious trouble and harm. In fact, it was fear of breaking her mother's heart that prevented her from crossing the line into more dangerous and potentially hazardous behaviors.

But when Judie's brother died, her brokenness drove her to search for the God she had never really known. For a year, God pulled at her heart, but she could not find Him.

Then one day a timid young lady walked up to Judie's door. The young lady was embarrassed and nervous; she was inviting a complete stranger to Bible study. But the Spirit had prepared Judie's heart. The moment she saw the young woman approaching her door, her heart leapt in her chest as John the Baptist leapt in Elizabeth's womb when Mary, who was carrying the Son of God, came to her door. Judie's enthusiastic response startled the reluctant visitor, but they were soon eagerly sharing with one another.

The Bible study fed Judie's heart, and her pain was eased as she encountered believers with dynamic faith. She was one of the youngest women in the group, and she was a new mother. It was at this study that she was exposed to the idea of praying for her children's future mates. These women of all ages prayed fervently for the spouses of their children and grandchildren, confident that these spouses were just the right ones because they had been prayed for so faithfully.

In her personal devotional time, with her sons playing at her feet, Judie prayed for their future wives. As her boys played with their toy cars and tractors, she imagined little girls playing with their dolls and animals. During those precious moments, those little girls became her daughters. She prayed, hoping they came from a Christian family for their own sakes.

Because Judie had not lived a Christian lifestyle as a young woman, she knew the transformative power of Christ, and she lived in confidence that her daughters-in-law, regardless of their backgrounds, would be the right ones for her sons. She prayed for their protection, both physical and emotional, and she asked God to help them. She even prayed for their love relationships, asking God to guard their hearts and not give too much of themselves away before meeting her sons. Mostly, she asked God to guide them and teach them to love Him with their whole hearts and souls.

From the moment her sons began bringing home girls, she decided they were perfect. She refused to look for their faults and failings; she supported her sons' decisions each and every time. Of course, not every girlfriend became a daughter-in-law. But because she couldn't possibly know which ones would become daughters, she chose to accept them all.

Judie realized that she couldn't begin relationships with these young women with a guarded and judgmental heart and then open her heart to them if they married her sons. No, it had to start from the moment she met them in order to keep her from hurting her future daughters-in-law.

Judie's oldest son met a beautiful young woman early in high school. They fell in love and remain together today. Their search was short and their love long-lasting.

Her second son dated different girls throughout high school and into college. Then he met a girl, and the two of them fit together like pieces of a puzzle. As puzzles go, the shapes that fit together usually are very different; the sides that interlock are completely opposite in form. However, when the pieces lock together, they reveal a better view of the overall picture of the puzzle itself.

This girl grew up in a large family with stern parents who loved their children but did not attend church or actively participate in the Body of Christ. Then, when she was a young teenager, her parents suddenly decided to attend church regularly. It wasn't long before she encountered the Savior. Her siblings, however, doubted the love and forgiveness of God. They couldn't grasp the concept of a loving God.

For some reason, this girl believed it. It was as if she always knew she was lovable and finally found that God was the one who loved her. She recognized the heart of God immediately, even though she had little exposure to Him, the Bible, or church in her early life. When she went away to college, she fell in love with Judie's son.

Upon her engagement, her future mother-in-law told her, "I've been praying for you since you were born. I prayed God would put a hedge of protection around you, that you would know His love and believe in Him." Like a flash of lightning, the girl knew that this was the reason she recognized her Savior's face when she met Him. He had been there all along, covering her with His wings and sheltering her from the harms of the world.

Judie's youngest son is still unmarried. But she prays for her future daughter continually. She is not an illusion or a phantasm of imagination, but a real, breathing person who is prayed for each and every day.

Judie's new daughters are a natural part of the family now. The concept of "in-law" has disappeared; their relationship is defined by the love they share for their special men and for their gracious Lord.

Prayer: *Father, I lift up to you my children's spouses. Prepare a place in my heart for them.*

Thought for the Day: The love a mother has for her children's spouses is indeed lovely.

10

ENGRAVED ON HIS PALM

Sherrie Eldridge

I have engraved you on the palms of my hands.
—Isa. 49:16

That God would allow me to meet my birth mother was beyond my wildest adoptee dreams! After searching for seven years to no avail, I hired a professional who found her in two days.

Two weeks later my husband and I were on a plane bound for a glorious reunion. My heart felt like a balloon ready to burst. I didn't know what to expect. Would I laugh or cry? It was like a million emotions exploding at once. I laughed, then I cried, then I laughed.

Through social engagements, she kept me at arm's length for the first few days, but when my husband left on a business trip, I fantasized a precious mother-daughter time. I would present her with the photograph album the adoption professional had recommended. Beginning with my hospital footprints to current photos of my husband, children, and grandchildren, she would tell me how proud she was of me. Instead, she flipped through the pages, pushed the album aside, and brusquely announced that I was a cute baby.

My heart recognized rejection, but my head refused to believe it. This was the woman who said when looking at my first photo that I sent to her, "When I look at your sweet face, I just know that you're mine." From that time forward, it was awkward, like trying to fit a square peg into a round hole.

On the last day, when she drove me to the airport, she grabbed the steering wheel and with hot tears streaming down her cheeks screamed, "You don't know how hard it is to give up a baby! I've thought about you every day of my life!"

When I responded with joy that she hadn't forgotten me, she snapped, "Now you're happy that I'm sad!"

Upon leaving, I knew that the reunion had been far from perfect, but at least it was a start.

Later, when I called to thank her, it was obvious that something had changed drastically. Cruel words hit the core of my adoptee soul, yet simultaneously the familiar promise from Isa. 49:15-16 came to mind:

> Can a mother forget the baby at her breast and have no compassion on the child she has borne? Though she may forget, I will not forget you! See, I have engraved you on the palms of my hands; your walls are ever before me.

Jesus kept His promise to never leave or forsake me, even in the deepest pit of my greatest adoptee fear. He was in me, around me, under me, over me, and for me. His powerful presence and sweet comfort were deeper than anything life could ever throw at me.

For two years I tried to reconcile to no avail. I asked folks not to be mad at her, for she did not know what she was doing. Well-intentioned hospital staff told her when she gave me up to forget about me and go on with life as if nothing had happened. She had never learned to grieve her loss. So upon seeing me face-to-face, she realized that the baby she never saw, the child hospital workers named Baby X, was a real person, with a real life. It was too much for her, and she wasn't able to receive the love I longed to give her.

Even though there was no further contact, I clung to a thread of hope that I would see her again. Maybe my husband and I could fly to where she lived and take her for dinner. There would be no pressure—no unwelcome topics. It would just be one more opportunity to honor her, to thank her for giving the gift of life to me.

Recently that thread of hope broke when I learned she died two years ago. Profound sadness washed over me. Yet when I look in the mirror, I see her face, for I look exactly like her. When I look at my unique and unchanging fingerprints that God created while I was in her womb, I feel a sense of connection to her, made by my Sovereign Lord, who has chosen to touch my life by adoption for a purpose—His purpose.

It's true—I didn't have a peachy reunion as television often portrays. However, my birth mother's rejection sent me to my knees, where Jesus embraces me every day with strong arms and nail-scarred hands.

And I'm comforted to know that in addition to those scars, somehow my name is engraved on His hands.

Prayer: *Lord Jesus, thank you for the parents you gave me. Help me be a blessing to my children.*

Thought for the Day: Jesus' love and comfort are far greater than any hurt life hurls at us.

11

BECAUSE HE LIVES

Brenda Fowler

You know him, for he lives with you and will be in you.
—John 14:17

In May 2007 I was one of 275 ladies at a weekend retreat in Virginia Beach, Virginia. As we lifted our voices in praise, singing the song "Because He Lives," written by Bill and Gloria Gather, my thoughts raced back more than two decades earlier to a distant life.

In 1984 I had stood in a similar setting among many of the same ladies, lifting my voice as I declared the truth that He—my Savior—lives. Tears had streamed down my face as we sang the words. The seeds of the promise of that chorus were planted within my heart, ready to grow and mature.

In November 1983 life had become unbearable. I was at rock bottom. For months my husband of 17 years had been living in a depressed state. Today, because of education and openness, he would be diagnosed as manic-depressive or bipolar. But at that time, misunderstanding led to misdiagnosis.

My husband and I had entered that year with a viable business, a beautiful home, nice cars, and many of the luxuries of life. To say the least, we were young and very materialistic, with no thought of the Lord or His ways. "Grab all the gusto you can get" was the pervasive theme of our existence.

From all outside appearances, my husband and I seemed to be living on top of the world. But a bad decision turned our lives upside down. Almost overnight our means of income was gone. As a result of our losses and because of the mental illness that he suffered, my husband's self-esteem and confidence to move forward were totally destroyed.

The news of our financial crash came the week before Thanksgiving. Frankly, I did not see anything for which we could be thankful. As a matter of fact, I was filled with desperation. What were we going to do? I had a mentally ill husband who was devastated, and we were facing financial ruin.

I visited my brother-in-law to get some much-needed advice concerning business matters. It must have been obvious to him how anxious and desperate I was at that point. When we finished talking about our financial crisis, he looked intently at me and riveted my attention with what I thought at the time was a strange question. He asked, "Brenda, when was the last time you went to church?" Then he went on to say, "God and church might be what you're looking for."

His question stuck in my mind like a flashing neon sign. I knew there had to be help and answers somewhere. I found myself thinking, *I really do need to go to church and to pray again. I need God's help.*

When I was a young girl my family attended church sporadically. As a teenager I had responded to the pastor's invitation at the close of a service and gone forward to pray. But unfortunately, I did not live out my commitment to the Lord. Even though I continued to feel His hand reaching out to me and knew that He had placed a call upon my life, I played the prodigal daughter and walked away.

After my brother-in-law's question, I began to think, *Maybe I could go back to church.* I couldn't get that possibility out of my mind, so the following Sunday I found my way to church.

When the invitation was given at the end of the service, I nearly ran to the altar. I fell on my face and draped myself across that wooden refuge, pouring out my heart to the Lord. As I prayed that morning, I came to realize anew that a Thanksgiving feast had been prepared for me by my Heavenly Father. Gratefully, I accepted His invitation. This prodigal was welcomed home with open arms.

In January 1984, just six weeks after accepting the Lord as my Savior, I came home one snowy afternoon and found that my husband had committed suicide.

I cannot begin to express the anguish of planning his funeral and consoling our 14-year-old son, Greg, as I waded through the financial maze over the following weeks and months. At the age of 34 I was suddenly a widow and single mom. I felt lost, alone, and abandoned. It seemed that everything we had worked for was gone. I found myself on the edge of bankruptcy. What did the future hold for Greg and me? What could I do—where could I turn? There were so many unanswered questions.

I clung to my Thanksgiving Sunday commitment to the Lord. Within my church the ladies embraced me with support and encouragement. Somehow we got through those days with my Heavenly Father's help. My new church friends rallied around me. Greg and I were going to make it, although our future looked very uncertain.

In God's divine plan, that May I was invited to a retreat for ladies from across Virginia. As I stood in the midst of my new-found friends, many unanswered questions raced through my thoughts. I had truly begun to realize that God would get me through. But I needed to hear from Him that Saturday morning. I prayed, *Father, could you give me a promise?*

Then we began to sing that beautiful promised-filled song the Gaithers had written. I had never heard those words before that morning. They rang out loud and clear as they fell into my heart like seeds into fertile soil. And then we got to the chorus. It was as though those words had been penned just for me. They permeated my very being.

In the following days, those words took root as they grew and matured in my life. My Heavenly Father gave me hope and a future. Now I knew who held the days ahead. As with Job, He has restored my life, multiplying my blessings many times over. I learned to devour the Bible, reading His promises, clinging to them, and feeling His hand upon me guiding my life.

A couple of years afterward, the Lord sent Tom into my life. We were married a few months later. Surely God had answered my prayers by sending Greg and me a wonderful husband and father, as well as David, a great stepson for me and stepbrother for Greg. And the Lord added great extended family members as well.

In 1984 I sang "Because He Lives" with a questioning but searching heart that was learning to trust. In 2007 I sang with a *knowing* heart.

And I agree with Job, who declared in Job 19:25, "I know my Redeemer lives."

Prayer: *Father, this day plant within my heart seeds of hope. Because you are alive, I have the promise of a future ordered by your divine plan.*

Thought for the Day: We can trust in the living Savior, who has promised to give us all we need for each day.

12

THOSE WHO CAME BEFORE US

Cheri Fuller

Likewise, teach the older women to be reverent in the way they live,
not to be slanderers or addicted to much wine, but to teach
what is good. Then they can train the younger women to love
their husbands and children, to be self-controlled and pure,
to be busy at home, to be kind, and to be subject to their
husbands, so that no one will malign the word of God.
—Titus 2:3-5

During Thanksgiving week I thanked God many times for women who came before me and taught me so much. Corrie ten Boom is one of those women. When I meet her in heaven, I'll thank her because my faith has been strengthened by her wise words and her example.

As a young woman I was impacted by her book and the movie based on it, *The Hiding Place*, which tells the story of how God sustained this small Dutch woman through the horrors of the Nazi concentration camp after she and her family were captured and imprisoned for hiding and caring for Jewish people during World War II. From the time of her release at the end of the war to her death in 1983, Corrie traveled the world, sharing a message of love, faith, and forgiveness.

From Corrie ten Boom's writings, I learned to stop focusing on my situation or problem and focus my mind on the Lord. "Keep looking in the right direction in everything you do—to Jesus; keep looking up and kneeling down," she taught us. "We are not ready for the battle until we have seen the Lord, for Jesus is the answer to all problems" (Corrie ten Boom, *Reflections of God's Glory*).

From Edith Schaeffer I learned how important it is to make a home wherever we find ourselves, large or small. Her book *What Is a Family?* was a great inspiration to me in my years of active mothering and homemaking. In each place the Schaeffers lived—from a crowded little chalet in Switzerland where they began L'Abri ministry to the apartment near the Minnesota hospital where Francis received chemotherapy during his last months of life—they made a center of meaningful living and beauty and reached out to invite others to share what they had.

The writings of Amy Carmichael have shed light on my path as well. A missionary to India, Amy sensed God's call as a young woman but had no idea of the dangerous work that lay ahead—to save young girls from cult prostitution in Hindu temples. Through many times marked by material need, great pain, illness, attacks, and disappointment, Amy experienced God as her great refuge and wrote of the sheltering love of God, who is with us in all things. This courageous woman stepped faithfully into the darkness, trusting Him in every circumstance. From Amy I learned to be patient, waiting for God to answer prayer in His time and way, and that patient waiting means hoping and trusting in the face of all discouragement.

Flo Perkins was a widow of 75 when she and I, a 30-year-old woman, began a friendship. On many occasions she sat at my kitchen table, or I at hers, eating slices of banana bread I had made. Whenever we talked, Jesus always came into the conversation, because He was her best friend. She prayed for me, my husband, and my children as long as she was on the earth, and she encouraged me to go deeper in prayer—not just with words but also with actions.

For a season, a few of us young women met with her in her home once a week early in the morning. Flo had been going into God's presence for more than 50 years, and prayer was as natural to her as breathing. She took us in on her wings, and without teaching—in the very act of praying honestly, humbly, and perseveringly—we learned a great deal from her about the power and value of prayer.

My friend Patty Johnson has shared her wisdom with me at her kitchen table, and her prayers have meant the world to me. She has taught me about celebrating the gift of life with creativity, zest, and enthusiasm. When I was dreading my 50th birthday, feeling a bit over the hill, she told me I was about to enter my prime, the best years of a woman's life, which she called "the fabulous 50s." And you know what? Patty was right.

My mother has been gone for more than two decades, but her wisdom and sayings mentored me through the years—like one of the first verses she taught my four sisters and me: "Be kind and compassionate to one another, forgiving each other, just as in Christ God forgave you" (Eph. 4:32). How grateful I am for a mother who not only prayed for me and my siblings and her grandchildren, but whose love lives on far beyond her life!

Many of those who have gone before us—our mothers, mothers-in-law, older friends, and spiritual women who have left us a legacy in their writings—are master teachers. No matter our age differences, if we open our hearts and minds, our lives will be tremendously enriched. If we ignore what they have to offer, we're missing out on a great resource.

Look around today to those who have encouraged you, prayed for you, or who would love to share their journeys and wisdom with you. Don't forget to give thanks for them—and to them.

Prayer: *Thank you, Lord, for the host of women who have mentored me. May I "teach what is good" to the younger women you place in my life.*

Thought for the Day: Pass on the baton of faith that will last for all eternity.

OUR HEALING SHEPHERD

13

Joyce Williams

You anoint my head with oil.
—Ps. 23:5

Oh yes, 2006 was a year of "night seasons." I was in the hospital six times. The coronary care unit personnel got to know me on a first-name basis. That had not been a personal goal of mine! But I did get to pray with some of them. A highlight was leading the head nurse to the Lord one morning before I left the hospital.

In August I started feeling so bad that I went to the emergency room, and they told me I was having a mild heart attack. Miraculously, there was minimal heart damage. Once again, the cardiologist placed a stent and did angioplasty. That year I had a total of five stents and two angioplasties. To be totally honest, uncertainty and anxiety clutched my heart.

It was such a difficult time. Our dear friend Renae Ryan came to Wichita and spent several days with me at great personal sacrifice. I had to miss our oldest granddaughter, Cherie's, wedding in Florida. And I couldn't go to Nashville with Gene as we had planned, so I didn't get to spend time with our daughter Tami and our youngest granddaughter, Lauren. Besides, I spent my 62nd birthday by myself! I was lonely and literally "heartsick." The future seemed so uncertain.

One morning as I was having my devotions, I cried, *Father, I really need a promise. I know you're in control, and you're leading me along, but could I have a special word of hope from you?* As I was completing my Bible study a few minutes later, this promise from Jer. 30:17 jumped off the pages and into my heart: "I will restore you to health and heal your wounds." Wow! Once again, sweet assurance swept over me.

As I reflected back on the way the Lord had continuously given me just the encouragement I needed, leading me along through each crisis, I was overwhelmed with thanksgiving.

He had cared for us in 2006. In January we had spent two weeks in India. Then we had been in Israel for 10 days in March. I had spent several days in New York later that month writing a piece for *Decision* magazine.

In April, after I became aware of my health issues, I received an e-mail from Lynn Fagg in Roanoke, Virginia, telling me the Lord had awakened her in the middle of the night to pray for me a few weeks earlier. She enlisted the prayer group at church (my home church), telling them about her concerns. Several weeks later she found out about my health problems.

Then Marilyn Stewart called to tell me that while she was on a cruise on the Nile River in Egypt, the Lord had told her to pray for me. Kathy Slamp called from Oregon to tell me she had been on a ship off the coast of Alaska when the Holy

Spirit said, "Pray for Joyce." Another time Becky and Wayne Dunman called from Roanoke to ask, "Are you OK? We felt impressed to pray for you." They caught me in the emergency room of the hospital with chest pains. How reassuring to know our Heavenly Father was talking to friends about me— many times when I didn't even know I was in trouble in the first place!

The cardiologist had scheduled the second renal stent for October 23. Gene and I presented our Annual Day of Renewal for Pastors and Spouses for the preceding Thursday, October 19. A couple of weeks prior to that date, Gene had said, "Honey, I believe the Lord wants us to add a new dimension this year—a time of anointing and prayer for healing." He called four pastors and made arrangements.

On that Thursday, when Gene called for those four pastors and anyone who wanted to be anointed to come forward, they streamed down the aisles. And I led the way.

Pastor Kendall Franklin from Hutchinson, Kansas, anointed me and prayed, *Father, when Joyce goes in for this next stent, I pray that the doctor will say, "There are no blockages."*

Our dear friends Joe and Jennifer Zollinger came to me a little later that day and also prayed for my healing. So I had a double prayer blessing!

The following Monday I checked into the hospital. Once again I found myself shivering on that far-too-familiar but still scary and cold steel table in the cath lab. As my cardiologist watched the snaking catheter, he exclaimed, "I don't understand it. There are no blockages!" The exact words of Pastor

Kendall's prayer! Then he said, "Disconnect everything and send her home!"

Every test since then has turned out well. I'm still on lots of meds and battle some fatigue, but I have the assurance from our healing Shepherd that He is leading me along.

Even though none of us knows what mountains or valleys we may climb, we know He is guiding our steps. And during the roughest parts of the path, there are times that He picks us up and carries us close to His heart.

Our Healing Shepherd

On the dark lonely mountains
Of pain and uncertainty
I cry out to our Good Shepherd,
"Won't you come and rescue me?"

In the raging storms of life
And dark nights of near despair
He gently draws me to Him,
My burdens and fears to bear.

He carries me near His heart
And shares my deepest grief.
Through His love and compassion
Body and soul find sweet relief.

Like a lamb He holds me close
With His wounded, nail-scarred hands
And whispers, "I know your pain;
Your anguish I understand."

He takes up my heavy load
*   That's too much for me to bear.*
With love and great compassion
*   He reveals how much He cares.*

He soothes my anxious spirit;
*   And anoints me with healing balm.*
Then He draws me to His heart,
*   And my fears and pain are calmed.*

He's still our healing Shepherd
*   Who hears our faintest cry.*
There's no valley that's too deep
*   Nor mountain that's too high.*

He always comes to rescue us
*   From every fear and distress,*
Tucking us in faith's sweet harbor
*   Where in Him we quietly rest.*

—Joyce Williams

Prayer: *Thank you for carrying me safely through life's toughest times.*

Thought for the Day: Our Shepherd guides us into healing paths.

14 GRACE AND PONIES

Kendra Graham

It is by grace you have been saved, through faith—
and this not from yourselves, it is the gift of God—
not by works, so that no one can boast.
—Eph. 2:8-9

My husband, Wil, and I have three wonderful young children: Quinn, 2; Rachel, 4; and C. J., 6. Our home is full of laughter, chaos, and constant motion. You're welcome to come for a visit, but don't expect the place to sparkle! I'm in constant prayer for all three of our precious kids.

"Someday, I hope you have a child *just like you!*" my mom constantly told me as I was growing up.

I always replied, (but not out loud) "Good, I hope so, too, because then I'll have someone to play with who'll understand me!" Well, as you might guess, I've been blessed with that child—Rachel is just like me.

It seems that Rachel always wants to do the opposite of whatever C. J. and Quinn are doing. And once she makes a decision—even if it's wrong—she'll endure hardship to the very end rather than recant her choice. Like her mom, she's one strong-willed little girl!

Rachel is almost five and very bright. But every time the children and I talk about sin and the need for God's forgiveness, Rachel always speaks up and says, "Not me, Mommy! Jesus doesn't need to forgive me. My heart is clean—I've never been bad."

That statement is a great source of frustration for me, because many times just an hour earlier she has been punished for lying, disobeying, or hitting her brother. The list goes on.

Recently we quoted Eph. 2:8-9 at dinner each night for a couple of weeks. I always emphasized the fact that there is nothing we can do to earn heaven. We cannot be perfect enough no matter how hard we try. So God provided a solution for us through the death of Jesus. And because of His grace, all we have to do is confess our sins and ask Him to forgive us. When He forgives us, we know we'll be with Him in heaven some day.

For two months I had been trying to get our sweet but determined Rachel to stop sucking her fingers. Rachel has about 40 tiny toy ponies in her beloved pony collection. Finally I told her that each time I caught her with her fingers in her mouth, I would take away a pony. I thought surely that would keep her from sucking those fingers. Nope. It seemed Rachel was almost more determined than ever to show me I had not gotten to her. Consequently, within two weeks I had all 40 ponies.

I put the ponies in the dining room so she would see them and be reminded that if she stopped grazing on her fingers,

69

the ponies would be hers again. Rachel was sad and would tell me in her soft, Southern accent, "I *can't* do it, Mamma!"

I would remind her, "But you have to—or no ponies."

While praying for Rachel during my quiet time one day, it was as if God leaned out of heaven and spoke to me about her. He seemed to whisper, *Give her the ponies—by grace!*

The *ponies? By grace?* A light went on. *Thank you, Lord!* Truly God knows our kids a lot better than we do.

The next day, when all three kids were screaming and running circles outside, I called Rachel to the steps to talk to her. When I asked, "Rachel, would you like to have *all* your ponies back?" she replied, "Oh, yes, Mommy!"

Then I asked, "Rachel, do you deserve to have them back?"

She replied, "No."

I continued. "Why not?"

She said, "Because no matter how hard I try I can't stop sucking these fingers!"

I said, "That's right! Rachel, you don't deserve your ponies. But I want to show you how grace works. If you just ask for your ponies, you can have them again—*all* of them, even though you don't deserve them! That's grace."

I went on to explain: "It's grace that enables us to get to go heaven too! If we just ask God to forgive us, He will. We don't deserve it, but if we really mean those words, He wipes our sins away. We get what we don't deserve."

Rachel's little eyes lit up, and she said, "Ohhh!" I asked her if she was ready to ask for her ponies back. She actually thought about it for a few seconds, and then said, "Oh, yes!"

So I gave them to her. At dinner that night she prayed, thanking God for grace even though she doesn't deserve it—and for her ponies.

That day Rachel learned that God's grace is truly the best gift we can ever receive—even better than her ponies.

Prayer: *Lord, give me guidance and wisdom to teach my children about you in every aspect of their lives.*

Thought for the Day: The grace of God is undeserved, unearned, but completely attainable—if we just ask.

15

HAPPY MEALS

Liz Curtis Higgs

A happy heart makes the face cheerful.
—Prov. 15:13

Hubby Bill and I thought our family food skirmishes would end when our two kids grew out of highchairs and started chewing solid foods. Silly us. Children who can read a menu are 10 times more dangerous.

"Look, Mom! They serve sweetbread."

Firm shake of the head. "You don't want that, honey. Trust me."

"I do, too!" Serious pouting. "Sweetbread is like Grandma's dessert cake, right?"

Motherly sigh. "No, it's like the pancreas of a calf."

"Ohhh." Eyes widen, face pales. "Can we go to McDonald's?"

I've tried waving away the offered menu with a smile and a simple question for the waiter: "What do you have that looks like a hot dog?"

"A hot dog, ma'am."

"Perfect. We'll take two, please. Plain. On buns."

Breakfast on the town is especially tricky if your kids aren't egg-eaters and the only pancakes they trust are yours. I've been known to hide Pop Tarts in my purse and pass them under the table with strict instructions to eat them wrapped in a napkin—preferably while wearing dark sunglasses.

Not all restaurant jaunts are so easily handled. Sometimes parents are reduced to one of three desperate appeals:

Stewardship. "We paid $12.95 for that eggplant casserole, son, and we're not leaving until you eat every bite. I know you thought the eggplant would be purple, but you're going to have to finish it anyway. Use your fork, please."

Starving children. "There are hungry children in [favorite Third-World country here] who would be very grateful to have that braised beef liver. No, we can't mail it to them—because it would spoil. Yes, fine—we'll send money. Now *eat!*"

Just one bite. "How will you ever know what food tastes like unless you try it? One little bite won't kill you, sweetie. Watch Mommy! Mommy is tasting your yummy oatmeal. Oh, isn't this nice? I know it's cold and lumpy and the color of wallpaper paste, but it's so-o good for you. See how Mommy is smiling?" *Glurp.*

My husband, Bill, has a theory about children and taste buds. He believes that sometime during a child's early years a mysterious 15-minute window opens. Whatever you feed the child while that window is ajar becomes his or her favorite food—forever.

Your picky daughter won't eat a thing? She was napping

during those critical 15 minutes. Sorry. Better luck next child. Your not-so-choosy kid eats the house down, from cucumber salad to mincemeat pie? His window flew open during a church potluck.

My own children were home alone with their father—horrors!—when their taste windows cracked open for those all-too-brief minutes. Hence, Lillian's favorite item is ketchup, which isn't even a food. Dill pickles were her other fave. Ketchup and pickles smooshed together are fine, too. Matthew's food-for-life is salsa. He won't eat any of the individual vegetables found in salsa, of course. But cook those tomatoes, peppers, onions, and garlic into oblivion, pour the remains in a jar, give it a name like "Hotter'n Blue Blazes," and he's a salsa-eating fool.

(I like salsa, too, but my brand is called "Wimpy, Wimpy, Wimpy.")

Matt recently came home from a church event and announced, "Tonight our youth group leader told us we're allowed one 'hate food'—something you aren't even allowed to put on my plate."

"Oh?" I gave him the mother eyebrow. "And yours would be ...?"

"Carrots—of course."

Of course. I'd been slicing, serving—then tossing out those orange veggies for years to no avail.

"You get to change your hate food once a year, on your birthday." Matt's smile was the length of a full-size carrot. "We learned that at church." Great.

Remember the four food groups we learned in Home Ec: fried, canned, frozen, and boxed? We parents know the real ones by heart: burgers, fries, little chicken thingies, and shakes. As long as those tried-and-true friends are on the menu, lunch on the road has a fighting chance.

But if fast food's always a hit, foreign food's always a miss. Believe me—we've tried them all. At a German restaurant we begged them to serve the wiener schnitzel on a bun so we could assure the kids it was a hamburger. Nein.

At the Mexican place, the only thing our children ate was the corn chips and salsa. At the Italian ristorante, it was nothing but bread. An Asian buffet? A no go—except for the fortune cookies. Try Greek, you say? They bravely partook of the ice water. Thai? Oh my.

On a family vacation, we discovered that even a Canadian meal can put our kids' taste buds to the test.

Canada's Cape Breton Island has much to offer—breathtaking vistas, fabulous fiddle music, and friendly folk in every small village. In Baddeck, one such town, a favorite feast of locals and tourists alike is the lobster supper. The all-in-one price included a huge lobster plus all the seafood chowder, steamed mussels, fresh biscuits, and tangy coleslaw a body can consume. For Bill and me, this was gastronomical heaven. For Lilly and Matt, it was—well, the other place.

There were no menus or choices to be made, save one: Non-lobster-eaters could enjoy a big slice of ham instead. Lucky for us, ham was on the children's acceptable food list. "Two hams, two lobsters," we ordered, grinning broadly in anticipation of the legendary meal headed our way.

To our right, the beautiful waters of Baddeck Harbour beckoned outside. To our left stood an aquarium brimming with live lobsters, their destinies certain. Minutes later, an enormous platter sat before us, boasting two bright red crustaceans, drawn butter by their sides, our tools of destruction gleaming by our plates.

The children took one terrified look at our dinners, then looked down to their tamer servings of ham as Bill and I took up our weaponry. Snap! Crunch! Rrrip!

Bibbed and dripping with buttery morsels of lobster, we tackled our much-touted maritime feast with gusto, tossing spare parts into the large plastic bucket planted in the middle of our table. It soon resembled a bizarre sort of centerpiece, filled with tails, claws, and other less recognizable post-consumer material.

It was while I was wrestling with a particularly stubborn bit of claw that I noticed how quiet things had become. Lilly and Matt were hunched over, hardly eating, with one hand shading their eyes.

"Is something the matter with your food?" Matt's head shook, but his hand never moved. Clearly he was trying to avoid seeing the mayhem occurring on our side of the table. Lillian, meanwhile, started to sniffle.

I reached out to pat her hand sympathetically. "Honey, it's OK. These lobsters aren't alive, like those in the tank." Bad move, Mom.

"Waahh!" Lilly's tears quickly shifted from a light rain to a downpour. Diners at half a dozen nearby tables stared at us in disgust. What were we doing to our daughter? Bill chose that moment to toss the head of his lobster into the white bucket, muttering, "I can't find a thing worth eating here."

It landed at a jaunty angle, leaving its tentacles waving above the bucket's edge. Lillian took one look and collapsed over her plate, her wail soaring an octave higher. Even Matt seemed a bit green around the gills. "Uh, can we leave now?"

"Leave?" Bill and I whined in chorus, seeing our long-awaited Baddeck lobster supper drowning in a sea of salty tears over a dimwitted, red-clawed critter.

We finished quickly, feeling more like cannibals with every passing second, and headed for the door, avoiding eye contact with the other patrons who muttered something about "those poor American children" even as their parents became poorer still at the cash register.

"How was everything?" the cheery proprietor asked, slamming the drawer shut on a goodly portion of our vacation funds.

"Delicious," said easy-to-please Bill.

"Fine," said anxious-to-leave Liz.

"OK," said ever-agreeable Matt.

"Awful!" sobbed ever-honest Lilly.

We left, still bibbed, and spent the next hour assuring Lillian that her parents weren't cannibals and that, yes, lobster could be her hate food—not just until her next birthday but for the rest of her natural, marine-creature-loving life.

Prayer: *Father, please help me find the happy side of adventures with my children.*

Thought for the Day: Laugh lines don't count as wrinkles!

16 ENFORCING THE LAW

· Aletha Hinthorn

As God's chosen people, holy and dearly loved, clothe yourselves with compassion, kindness, humility, gentleness and patience.
—Titus 3:4

At the end of a summer day when my children were young, I was thoroughly frustrated. Why were Gregg, aged 14, and Arla, aged 7, continually fussing with one another? My reaction was to be upset with both of them. While considering this unpleasantness, I read Prov. 31:26: "She openeth her mouth with wisdom; and in her tongue is the law of kindness" (KJV).

This lady of Prov. 31 had a law: only kind words would pass from her lips. She was not all smooth and smiling, courteous and sweet with others, then frowning, cross, and discontented at home. A law that really works is constant and consistent.

Could I make kindness a law on my tongue? I wondered. I had heard of a mother frustrated with her son who pulled over the grocery store's candy bar rack. The little boy, thoroughly shaken and warned by his mother not to move a muscle, kept his gaze on her while quietly reaching for his blanket. He completely relaxed once his thumb was in his mouth and he held the comforting blanket in his hand. That blanket had always been gentle to him. How I longed to be as free from harshness as that blanket so I could be a haven for my children.

I determined to enforce the law of kindness on my tongue. My children would get enough hard knocks in life without receiving any from me.

My determination was rewarded by Gregg's comment the following day. "Know what day has been the most fun of the summer? Yesterday." The list of activities had not been spectacular: lunch at Taco Via, a shopping trip to buy a tennis racquet, and a visit to a school playground.

But I had made a discovery. My children reflected my attitude. When Arla irritated Gregg—easy enough for a little sister to do—he was cross. I then reacted by scolding them. When I quit reacting, Gregg and Arla became more tolerant of each other. Our unhappy episodes nearly disappeared when their behavior failed to trigger a disagreeable response from me. If I could react with kindness, they seemed to be able to be kind also.

In the days ahead, if my children showed bad attitudes, I looked at them as though they were mirrors of me and wondered what attitude of mine they were reflecting. It also helped me realize that although I must handle their immediate problems firmly, in the long run they would be helped only as I consistently kept the law of kindness on my tongue. It wasn't enough to act calm and patient—I had to feel gentle because they sensed my spirit and responded to that.

I so wanted kindness to be on my tongue that I gradually changed my habits. It wasn't automatic or without remissions. I found I had to continually pray for the mind of Christ.

One day when Arla was 14 and she and I were cooking in the kitchen, she asked, "Mom, are you ever impatient?"

"What did you say?" I asked, and she repeated the question.

"Well, if you don't know . . ." My words trailed off. Perhaps it's just that teens forget easily and we had enjoyed some pleasant days. I was encouraged, though, to keep trying to apply the law of kindness.

Prayer: *Thank you, Jesus, for enabling me to deal with troublesome situations. I praise you for your constant kindness to me.*

Thought for the Day: Our children reflect our attitudes.

BLINDED BY THE LIGHT

17

Lyndell Hetrick Holtz

He has not dealt with us after our sins;
nor rewarded us according to our iniquities.
—Ps. 103:10, KJV

As a mother, pastor's wife, and Christian, I thought the last thing I would do would be to commit adultery. Yet during a season of spiritual and marital emptiness, Satan ensnared me with his crafty lies. Eventually I faced ruin to such an extent that I was certain even God had abandoned me.

Perhaps that's why a scene in the movie *Seabiscuit* never fails to bring tears to my eyes. After several minor victories, Seabiscuit, a racehorse, was entered in a high-stakes race and favored to win. And he almost did. Thinking he had it in the bag, Red—a has-been, emotionally crippled jockey—eased up on the reins while being blindsided by another horse and rider. Seabiscuit lost by a nose.

Afterward the trainer, Tom, cornered Red and berated him for slacking off while a rider was flanking him on the right. Red interrupted Tom's tirade, yelling, "I didn't see him! I can't see out there!"

Realizing what Red just revealed, Tom stormed out and found Charles, the owner: "He lied to us! He can't see! He's *blind* in his one eye!" A shocked silence hung between them as they digested the ramifications of such news.

Since Red's deception naturally warranted the end of his career, Tom asked, "What do you want to do with him?"

Charles hesitated, and then with a grace-filled smile he said, "You don't throw a whole life away just because it's banged up a little."

Eight years ago, like Red, sin had left me emotionally and *spiritually* crippled. Having eased up on the reins of faith due to *spiritual* blindness, Satan blindsided me and led me down the dead-end road of adultery. Eventually my detour ended in shame and humiliation, bringing unimagined loss and devastation to my husband, children, and our church. Like Red, my life was severely banged up, and I knew I deserved to be discarded. Yet I longed for what no finite being could offer—I desperately needed God's smile of *infinite* love and grace to assure me that He had not tossed this banged-up life away.

But I had a problem. God's love had always been foreign to me—not to my head but to my heart. As a result, my disillusionment over God's love for me greatly intensified as I struggled to receive His forgiveness for what I had done. I could not get past the idea that a disgusted God had given up on me.

But one day it all came to a head—the day my husband packed up and drove away, bringing an end to 25 years of history together. I walked through the door and could go no farther. Dropping to the floor, I wept in anguish and disbelief. For five months we had tried to salvage our marriage, and I could not believe it had come down to this—me wailing like a madwoman on the kitchen floor and David driving like a madman far away from me. I could not believe that my marriage was over, that my husband was gone! *This was not what I had wanted!*

Alone and shattered, I resumed my daily pleading with God to touch me with a *heart* knowledge of His love and forgiveness, for I was convinced that I would not make it without such assurance. But again the old, familiar darkness of unbelief that God could love someone as marred as me rose up like the walls of Jericho. They seemed impenetrable.

In a now-or-never moment, I picked up my Bible and opened it at random. My eyes fell directly to this passage:

He has not dealt with us according to our sins, nor rewarded us according to our iniquities. For as the heaven is high above the earth, so great is His mercy toward those who fear Him. As far as the east is from the west, so far has He removed our transgressions from us *(Ps. 103:10-12, KJV).*

Like a broken dam, the light of truth—that Jesus had died in the place of one who deserved death—flooded my soul. As He tenderly held my heart in His hand, I heard Him say, *If you're waiting for more proof than this of my love for you, you'll wait in vain. For there's no greater love than the fact that I died for you when you loved me not.*

The walls came tumbling down. Tears of anguish turned to sobs of wonder and joy as God's love pushed back my darkness. My heart finally knew. Jesus and the Cross are proof that

God will never throw a whole life away just because it's banged up a little.

Eight years later, this banged-up life is a broken vessel that now shines with the treasure of God's transforming love. Not only has my life been restored, but my home has been restored as well. Three years after our divorce, God's love brought healing to a shattered marriage. Over time, a husband's forgiveness was granted, vows were renewed, and love was reborn.

God's healing love has overflowed from our marriage into the hearts and lives of our four banged-up adult children. Though the losses were many during my spiritual and matrimonial mutiny, the greatest loss belonged to our children. During this time they made decisions that became the source of today's consequences. Yet I'm awestruck at the way God's love is performing miracles in their lives since my husband and I remarried five years ago.

In spite of the years I sacrificed to the swarming locusts, God has kept His promise—He has not dealt with me according to my sins. Instead, His love has been unleashed to every area of my life. And as I look at the vast distance between the stain of my transgressions and what God has accomplished in my life, my marriage, and in our children's lives, I'm left happily and incurably blinded by the light of His amazing love.

Prayer: *Thank you, Father, for seeking me in the darkness of my sin and enfolding me in the light of your love.*

Thought for the Day: Sin cannot take us so far that God's grace cannot reach us.

18 FAITH IN LIFE'S VALLEYS

Shirley Hostetler

I can do everything through him who gives me strength.
—Phil. 4:13

There's no way I could have imagined surviving the loss of both my children. Thank God—I was blessed to have grown up in a loving Christian family with parents who always trusted God. Watching them handle tough times gave me a great pattern to follow. When I was young, Dad gave me Phil. 4:13, promising me that God would enable me to do all things. That became my life verse.

Not long after graduating from nursing school, I married and began working as a nurse. A few years later, our daughter, Tammy, was born, followed by our son, Troy, three years later. Life seemed good.

Then, just before Christmas 1979, my husband came home and said, "I don't love you anymore—probably never have loved you. I want a divorce." Although I prayed and cried out to God, the divorce was finalized. I held onto God's promise that Dad had given me. *Was divorce included in all things?*

It was hard to witness my children's pain caused by the divorce and their father's rejection. Tammy turned to food for comfort, which resulted in health problems that eventually damaged her organs. Troy handled things by wanting to prove to everyone he could be successful. Somehow the Lord provided for both of them to graduate from college.

Tammy's weight continued to spiral out of control. After many job rejections, she finally accepted a teaching assignment on the Hopi Reservation in Arizona. The people loved and accepted her.

Troy worked in Kansas City as he and his fiancé, Dana, made wedding plans. Tammy came home during the summer of 1994, and we had fun making wedding decorations. In October she returned for the wedding. Although we had a wonderful time, she was very quiet and withdrawn. When I took her to the airport, she cried as we hugged goodbye.

Her health continued deteriorating. When we talked on Sunday, November 27, 1994, she didn't sound like herself. I kept a running conversation with God, *What more can I do for Tammy? How can I help her?*

Finally, early in the morning of November 29, I cried out to God, *Only you can heal her. I give her back to you.*

I was at work later that morning when the phone call came, a mother's worst nightmare: Tammy had been found dead in her bed. She had died at 5:00 A.M., the time I had released her. I couldn't believe she was gone. My pain and heartbreak were beyond description.

God ministered to me through my family and friends. I

learned more than I had ever thought I would need to know about Phil. 4:13.

Troy and Dana blessed our lives with a grandson, Caden, who brought so much joy. Life began to look brighter. Then, in January 1999, my beloved father died of a massive heart attack. I clung to the promise he had shared with me—"all things."

In December 2000 Troy and Dana told me I was going to be a grandma again. What a joy! Life began to feel good. In January 2001 I attended a ladies' retreat. The speaker, Joyce Williams, seemed to have just the words I needed to hear. Afterward I kept reading again and again the verses and thoughts. Little did I know that in three days my world would once again crash around me.

I was at work when I was notified that Troy had been killed in an automobile accident! I couldn't believe it. I had been faithful. I had remained steadfast. How could I give up my last child? I thanked God for Dana and Caden and the promised new grandson. But my heart was broken with the loss of both my children.

I kept turning to my life verse. Could I truly do all things? Even lose my only two children? Once again, I found solace in the promises of God, my family, and friends.

On June 5, 2001, Carson was born. It was a bittersweet day. The pain of loss and the joy of new life resulted in an emotional rollercoaster. Dana and the boys continued to be such a blessing to me. She made a secure, happy home for them. I got to keep the boys as often as I wanted.

I rejoiced when God brought a wonderful new man named Mike into Dana's life. It was so good to see her smiling again. Both boys escorted Dana down the aisle, and Caden gave her away when they were married in June 2003. We love Mike. He is a great husband and father.

My life goes on. Although God has guided me in paths I would not have chosen, I have grown closer to Him. I remember what I heard at the retreat just three days before Troy died: "Joy is not the absence of suffering but the presence of God." I have found that to be true.

Today I can tell others who face tragedies that we can truly do all things through Him—because He always gives us strength—just when we need it.

Prayer: *May I always lean on your strength—not my own.*

Thought for the Day: The Lord is always faithful to give His sustaining power.

19

BELOVED DISCIPLE: "BIDDY" CHAMBERS

Joyce Williams

Let the beloved of the Lord rest secure in Him.
—Deut. 13:12

Nicknames interest me. So I was intrigued when I read that Oswald Chambers lovingly designated his dear wife and soul mate as the "beloved disciple." Then he shortened that nickname to the initials *B.D.* and then affectionately to *Biddy*. And that's what she was called the rest of her life.

If ever there was a match made in heaven, it was when the Lord brought those two together. They met while he was traveling and speaking for the League of Prayer in Britain, and they were married in 1908.

Biddy Chambers had already been trained as a court stenographer before she met Oswald. She could take shorthand faster than most people could talk. From the beginning, when she listened to her husband's messages, she took shorthand notes— reams of them—having no idea that one day she would be transcribing them into 50 books written by Oswald Chambers.

Shortly after they were married, Oswald became principal of the newly opened Bible Training College (BTC) in London, sponsored by the League of Prayer. Biddy filled many roles as lady superintendent by overseeing multiple logistical details. In addition to teaching, she prepared meals, provided temporary housing for missionary families, as well as transcribing Oswald's lectures.

As her husband taught, Biddy sat in the back of his class-rooms and chapel services recording his words verbatim. Because they were so in tune with each other, she was able to capture the essence of his messages into a priceless store-house of notes that multiplied daily.

Kathleen, their only child, was born in 1913 and soon became the darling of BTC. Oswald especially doted on his baby girl.

With the outbreak of World War I in 1914, BTC was closed. Oswald volunteered to work at a YMCA in Egypt, where he was joined by Biddy, Kathleen, and several of their former students from BTC. He soon established himself as a friend of the troops at Zeitoun Camp, near Cairo.

Biddy continued to fill shorthand notebooks with Oswald's messages to the troops. Although she battled the heat, the sand that constantly blew, and stinging insects, she created a homelike atmosphere for her family and the homesick troops.

Oswald adored his dear Biddy. They were an awesome, divinely ordained team working together to advance the Kingdom, regardless of their setting.

In late October 1917, Oswald had an emergency appendectomy and appeared to be recovering. Tragically, two weeks later, on November 15, he relapsed and died. Suddenly Biddy was a young widow in a foreign country with a four-year-old daughter. She sent a telegram to her family and friends saying simply, "Oswald in His presence."

Biddy and Kathleen remained in Egypt for two years as she worked with the troops. God miraculously blessed her transcription of one of Oswald's sermons that she personally sent as a Christmas gift to the troops in Egypt. Out of that evolved the monthly publication of 10,000 copies by the YMCA.

It wasn't long before Biddy realized that her true calling was to give her beloved husband's words to the world. Thus, she perpetuated their shared dream of working together to spread the gospel.

Biddy and Kathleen returned to England in 1919, and she continued transcribing reams of notes from Oswald's lectures. Kathleen later shared that her mother was always available to anyone who knocked at their door. She was always prepared to stop what she was doing to respond to someone in need. Biddy was the consummate mother to Kathleen and a friend to all.

To support herself and her daughter, Biddy opened a boarding house for students in Oxford while compiling *My Utmost for His Highest*. It was first published in 1927 and has become the world's bestselling devotional book, translated into more than 40 languages.

Truly, Oswald Chambers' books are the culmination of a great love story—the couple's love for God, for each other, and for others. Their ministry continues to impact lives many generations later.

By the time she died in 1966, Biddy had compiled and published 50 books under her husband's name. It is significant to note that her name was never mentioned. Throughout her life, she was convinced that her true calling was to give her husband's divinely inspired words to the world.

May all of us learn from this dearly beloved disciple, Biddy Chambers.

Prayer: *Father, teach me true humility that I, too, may become a beloved disciple.*

Thought for the Day: Those who humble themselves will be exalted by God.

20

A BLESSING OR A BURDEN?

Cynthia Spell Humbert

Behold, children are a gift of the Lord.
—Ps. 127:3, NASB

Motherhood was quite an adjustment for me. My husband, David, and I waited until I was 30 to have Elisabeth. At that point I had an established career as a Christian counselor, speaker, and author. I was naive enough to think that motherhood would be a breeze compared to all the busy hours of my hectic work schedule. I told myself that as soon as I quit work to stay home with the baby, I would have lots of free time. I pictured myself having long, quiet strolls with the baby in the park.

It seemed as if it was the hottest June in history, and my eighth months of pregnancy felt more like eight long years of being nauseated, fat, and ugly. It's at that point during pregnancy that you begin to care no longer how the baby comes out. You just want it over and to have your life back!

Little did I know that there would be days when I would think I had accomplished something if I got out of my pajamas and brushed my teeth before noon! Working was much easier than mothering. Before motherhood I slept more than three hours at a time, had a scheduled lunch break, could call in sick, and could even go to the bathroom alone. Being a mother quickly taught me that my life was no longer about me and that to be a good mother I needed to become a good servant. But let's face it—putting someone else's needs first isn't always easy.

One afternoon when Elisabeth was two years old, she had a friend over to play. I was pregnant and exhausted, so I felt grateful that she was sharing nicely with her little playmate. When I asked if they were ready for lunch, the kids both easily agreed to peanut butter and jelly sandwiches. So far, so good.

I don't know why children have an aversion to bread crust, but they do. Things were going just fine until I put the meal in front of them. Suddenly the whining broke out as Elisabeth said, "No crust, Mommy, no crust—pwease."

Of course, her friend, who shared the aversion, chimed in, "Me not want crust too." I took a deep breath.

As I stood at the kitchen counter, crying and cutting the crusts, David came home unexpectedly. He cheerfully asked, "Are you having a good day with the kids?" That is a dangerous question to ask a miserable, pregnant woman who's holding a knife.

I turned around as fast as a swollen mommy can. Tears flooded down my cheeks as I wailed, "This is not the way I planned my life!" Thrusting the sandwiches in his face, I cried, "For this crust I have two master's degrees."

My sweet husband didn't miss a beat as he hugged me and said, "But, Honey, you cut those crusts so much straighter than you ever could have with just one degree!"

Susanna Wesley had 19 children in 19 years. Can you imagine? The children knew she wanted to be alone whenever she pulled her apron over her head. I don't know about you, but if I had that many children, I would crawl back in bed and pull a *sheet* over my head! In my worst moment, I would probably say, "If you touch this sheet again, you're dead."

Jesus says that if you want to make a difference in the world, then serve His little ones. Every day as we serve our children, we're serving and honoring Jesus.

I'm now the proud mama of three children, and thankfully, none of them is still in diapers. I have learned that I can choose to think of my children as burdens or blessings. When I have a pity party and think I'm missing out on an opportunity, then I feel burdened with responsibility. But when I realize that God created each of my children uniquely and gave them all to me because He trusts me to shape their lives toward loving Him, then I can certainly see what treasures and blessings they are.

Prayer: *Lord, help me remember that the direction of the world can be changed through the sacrifices and prayers of godly mothers.*

Thought for the Day: There is no higher calling than that of motherhood.

21

WORTH PONDERING

Becky Hunter

Jesus grew in wisdom and stature,
and in favor with God and men.
—Luke 2:52

I think it would be fascinating to read Mary's diary to learn what the young Jesus did and didn't do. Jesus was perfect—He never sinned. But any young boy's energy and antics, even sin-free ones, can keep a mother busy! If we knew Mary's reactions to her Son's maturity or occasional lack thereof, would it have an impact on the way we interact with our own children as they journey to adulthood?

Scripture highlights just two events concerning Jesus' early years as well as Mary's reactions to them. Both are found in Luke 2. These incidents, more than a decade apart, essentially bookend His childhood.

The first took place when Jesus was a newborn. The shepherds heard from an angel about the birth of Jesus, and after visiting the holy family and finding Jesus to be exactly as an angel described Him, they told everyone that the Savior, Christ the Lord, had been born. Mary heard what these men of the community had to say about her Son, and she "pondered them in her heart" (v. 19).

The second incident took place 12 years later. Mary and Joseph couldn't find their preteen Son and spent three days looking for Him. When they finally located Jesus, they expressed their concern about not being able to find Him. His response? "Didn't you know I had to be in my Father's house?" And with that, Mary no longer pondered what the community had to say about who Jesus was as much as she tried to figure out what Jesus was trying to get *her* to understand about who He is.

As our children mature, we, too, move from relying mostly on information from others about who they are to learning from our sons and daughters about who they understand themselves to be. We can gauge their maturity by recognizing what their responses say about them. As they choose to respond to God and His calling on their lives, they're reaching levels of maturity that will carry them throughout their lifetimes.

Scripture's profound silence on the details of how Jesus was brought up actually makes sense to me. God surely had good reasons for leaving them out. Maybe including them would have limited some cultural and generational creativity that God hopes we can enjoy. We need only look around us to see how much God loves differences!

But even beyond that, if there were a "How to raise another child like Jesus" checklist penned by Mary, I would not have been alone in attempting to follow it. And I would have failed miserably—not just because none of my children is Jesus, but also because I would have been more focused on Mary's "formula" than on training my children in the way *they* should go.

So instead of a formula, the Bible gives us even more valuable information: In Luke 1:47 we find Mary's spirit rejoicing in God her Savior. Rejoicing in God her Savior went a very long way in making Mary a wonderful woman and mom. Rejoicing in God my Savior will go a long way in making me godly and effective in my roles as well.

Two thousand years ago Mary took the following verses to heart, just as we have the privilege of doing today:

Love the LORD your God with all your heart and with all your soul and with all your strength. These commandments that I give you today are to be upon your hearts. Impress them on your children. Talk about them when you sit at home and when you walk along the road, when you lie down and when you get up *(Deut. 6:5-7)*.

If we do discover someday that Mary "blogged" on papyrus scrolls, I'll be intrigued. But my guess is that she chose to leave the commentary to others and that she spent her precious time sharing with her young Son about His Heavenly Father.

Prayer: *Lord, through every stage of my children's lives help me love you well and live in ways that honor you. Help me train them in the way they should go, pointing them always in your direction.*

Thought for the Day: The best gift we can give our children is to tell them about their Heavenly Father.

22

32 ROSES

Sarah Johnson

The God of all grace, who called you to his eternal glory in Christ,
after you have suffered a little while, will himself restore you
and make you strong, firm and steadfast.
—I Pet. 5:10

I had just poured my morning cup of coffee when I noticed I had a message on my answering machine. I totally forgot my coffee as I was riveted by the words of the soft-spoken woman with a Southern accent. Grasping the telephone in a death grip, I listen intently as she introduced herself. Then she explained she was calling from the State of Tennessee Children's Services Post-Adoption Unit. She asked me to return her call.

My hands began to shake as I sat down and called the number. When I reached her, I couldn't believe my ears. She told me the son we had given up for adoption was searching for us. She was calling to confirm that I was his birth mother. I had prayed and dreamed about this call for 32 years. My heart beat like a hammer!

I explained I had married Dale, our son's birth father. I was 16 and Dale was 19 when I had given birth to our precious son. I had married someone else several years afterward, and that marriage ended in divorce. Then Dale and I reconnected. I explained that we had been happily married for 18 years. We had four children, including two from my previous marriage.

I wanted to call Dale immediately but couldn't reach him. I called my sister, my mother, and my former pastor, Gene Williams, who had been involved in the adoption process. I shared how I had prayed one day our son would search for us.

When I finally reached Dale, I told him the wonderful news about our son. He was quiet for a moment, and I could sense his excitement. Our son wanted to contact us!

The rest of the day I couldn't seem to put one foot in front of the other. I had told our children when they were young that we had another child, so this news was not a shock to them. They were excited about the prospect of meeting their brother as well.

We completed the paperwork. Each night as I tried to sleep, I prayed, *Please, God! Please let us hear from our son.* Three weeks to the day after receiving that call, the phone rang while we were finishing dinner. I glanced at the caller-ID screen. An out-of-area number was displayed. My heart pounded as I picked up the phone. Then I heard that dear voice and those wonderful words: "Mrs. Johnson, my name is Benjamin Dale Holt. I believe I'm your son."

Our son! Tears filled my eyes. He thanked me for giving him life, assuring me that I had made the right decision. Then he told me about his wonderful Christian parents who had given him a good childhood. I was so relieved. He was delighted when I told him that his birth father and I were happily married and that he had a brother and three sisters.

As we chatted, he told me about his family—his wife, Deanne; daughters, six-year-old Abbey and seven-month-old Sadie. Dale and I were thrilled to find we had more grandchildren. He also said they had another daughter named Sarah who had lived only two days. My heart ached for them. But we were amazed they had named her Sarah—*my* name! Also, it was quite a surprise to know Ben's middle name was Dale.

I told Ben that many times over the years Dale, my mother, and I had tearful conversations about him and how we had prayed that someday God would bring him back into our lives. Our prayers had been answered!

We agreed we should meet. He asked if we had any plans for the following weekend. Two days later, Ben and his family arrived. It was amazing how much Ben looks like Dale. Their mannerisms are so similar. Abby looks similar to the way I did when I was a little girl.

We spent three glorious days answering Ben's questions and sharing stories. Everything felt so comfortable. It was exciting getting together with our children, grandson, grandmothers, aunts, and uncles.

When it was time to say good-bye, amidst the tears and hugs, I told Ben how over the years I had looked up at the moon, thinking of him and wondering if he was looking at it too. We thanked God for our new beginning. Before they left, we gave them a photo of all us together with a message that read, "Thank you for finding us."

Ben and his family left early the next day to return to their home in Murfreesboro, Tennessee. Later that day, a beautiful bouquet of 32 red roses arrived—a rose for each year of Ben's life. Tears of joy streamed down my face as I read the card: "Thank you for wanting to be found."

Now our family is complete.

Prayer: *Thank you, Father, for watching over lost children.*

Thought for the Day: God is in the restoration business!

23 MY REDHEADED ANGEL

Linn Kane

He will command His angels concerning you.
—Ps. 91:11

My Grandma Morgan was like a guardian angel to me. She was my biggest prayer warrior—standing in the gap for me as she prayed fearlessly along with my mother and father.

When I was diagnosed with learning disabilities as a young child, Grandma encouraged me and believed in me. Although the experts told my parents I would probably not be able to finish junior high school, Grandma always pushed me to achieve. Her vibrant red hair was a like a flaming torch that blazed the trail for me as she constantly challenged and motivated me.

With Grandma's and my parents' encouragement, I not only finished high school, but I also graduated from college with a bachelor's degree in behavioral science. It was my privilege to work for years with delinquent juveniles. Then I felt God wanted me to change fields and be trained in emergency medical services. Once again, Grandma cheered me on—encouraging me to follow my dream.

I went back to school and graduated this past May with a degree in emergency medical services. I am a nationally registered paramedic. I do ambulance and helicopter critical care, which covers just about everything from major trauma to cardiac incidents. My red-haired cheerleader rejoiced with me in every accomplishment.

When I got the news that Grandma had cancer, I was devastated. She suffered for several years, and then word came that she was nearing the end of her life. It was difficult being so far apart. She was in Wichita, Kansas, and I was in Bartlesville, Oklahoma. I traveled back and forth to visit Grandpa and Grandma many times during her illness.

Early Sunday morning, October 29, 2006, I awakened from a deep sleep. I lay there awestruck, reflecting on a very a vivid dream. I remembered finding myself in a bright, wonderful, indescribable light. It was warm, and I heard beautiful voices. An enormous multitude of people whose faces seemed too bright to behold was standing around, one person in the middle of the group. Somehow the crowd was parted down one side by an even greater, indescribably bright light. I knew that light was coming from the throne and that Jesus was at its center.

As I looked closer, I began to recognize some of those in the circle—former pastors, old friends, my paternal grandma, and my great-grandparents. Then somehow I saw Peter, Paul, Moses, Abraham, David, Daniel, and Ruth! There were so many I could not begin to list all of them. But my grandma stood right there in the middle of the circle, looking radiant, her red hair blazing. I suddenly realized that this was Grandma's welcome party in heaven. They were greeting her. She was finally home.

The dream had seemed so real that I didn't want to stop thinking about it. But I looked at my clock and realized I had to get ready for church. I hurriedly dressed, grabbed a bite of breakfast, and rushed out the door. I made it in time for choir practice and then sang with the choir in the service. When we finished singing, I slipped into the pew behind Mom and Dad. As I did, Mom turned around and whispered, "We just got a call—Grandma died early this morning."

As I sank into my pew, I was amazed. The time of her death was minutes before I awakened that morning. My dream was true—Grandma was home with the Lord. And, oh, did she have a welcoming party! My heart swelled within me as tears filled my eyes.

We hurriedly packed and drove to Wichita to be with Grandpa. The hours were filled with preparations. Although I was wrapped in the afterglow of my wonderful dream, I missed Grandma enormously. Reality was setting in.

After the memorial service the following Tuesday, we went out to dinner. We had forgotten that it was Halloween and were somewhat surprised to see the servers and staff dressed in costumes. When our waitress came to us, I was astonished. She was dressed like an angel. And her halo encircled a mass of flaming red curls.

I felt that although Grandma was gone, my Heavenly Father had sent His angels to watch over us. And He had even sent a redheaded angel to our table as a tangible reminder!

Prayer: *Thank you, Father, for surrounding me with your angels.*

Thought for the Day: God comforts each of us with His unique custom design.

24 LAYING OUR ISAACS DOWN
Carol Kent

When they reached the place God had told him about, Abraham built an altar there and arranged the wood on it. He bound his son Isaac and laid him on the altar, on top of the wood. . . . "Do not lay a hand on the boy," he said. "Now I know that you fear God, because you have not withheld from me your son, your only son." . . . So Abraham called that place The LORD Will Provide. And to this day it is said, 'On the mountain of the LORD it will be provided.'"
—Gen. 22:9, 12, 14

Sometimes we choose to make sacrifices; we tighten our belts to pay for the education of our children, or we give up a treasured day off to help a friend in need. And then there are sacrifices that are thrust upon us without warning or survival instructions—such as the one Abraham experienced in Gen. 22.

On October 24, 1999, my husband, Gene, and I faced the most horrifying crisis in our lives. The unthinkable had happened, and we found ourselves walking up the steep mountain of testing as never before.

Our only child, Jason P. Kent, was arrested and charged with first-degree murder. Jason is an Annapolis Naval Academy graduate with an exemplary record. He has been the greatest source of pride and joy to both of us. His gifts, talents, and accomplishments have been tremendous blessings in our lives.

Ultimately Jason was convicted and sentenced to life in prison without the possibility of parole. I share our story in my book *When I Lay My Isaac Down*. It's about discovering that the cup of sorrow is also the cup of joy as we engage ourselves in understanding the upside-down nature of the Cross. Through writing this book, I can give people the opportunity to find hope, and it's the perfect way for me to process my own grief.

Having to relive horrific circumstances as I reviewed news clippings of deep sadness and personal trauma was agonizing beyond description. Proving once again that our Heavenly Father always brings good things out of horrible situations, God gave us a new vision.

During that painful period when I was writing the book, Gene and I prayerfully decided to establish a nonprofit organization to positively impact prisons: Speak Up for Hope (<www.speakupforhope.org>). We came to realize that while God would never condone what our son did, His mercy and grace abound. Our eyes have been opened to a whole new world—the prison system. We now see needs of which we were never aware, and doors are opening to help some of the most down-and-out people in the United States

There are about 2,000 prisons in the United States and thousands of inmates in need. The primary goal of Speak Up for Hope is to bring to light needs that are not currently being addressed and to assist churches and organizations in adopting a prison to meet those needs. It has become very obvious to us that the needs of prisoners and their families proliferate, and no one organization can possibly meet them all. Speak Up for Hope also addresses prisoner family needs in a way that will complement existing nonprofit organizations.

Gene and I are determined to face the future with hope, joy, and faith. We continue to realize that it's astonishing what God can do. He can take a situation like ours and redeem it for His purposes. God is truly amazing!

Adapted in part from Carol Kent's book, *When I Lay My Isaac Down*, copyright 2004, NavPress, www.navpress.com.

Prayer: *Dear Heavenly Father, as I face the valleys and mountains of motherhood, help me feel your presence as you walk with me or even carry me through difficult times.*

Thought for the Day: The most empowering way to do battle is to lay down our weapons of anger and unforgiveness and embrace God's relentless love.

25 RUBIES ARE A GIRL'S BEST FRIEND

Vicki Lancaster

A wife of noble character who can find?
She is worth far more than rubies.
—Prov. 31:10

I love Proverbs 31—well, at least *now* I do. When I first read it I was a little confused. I thought the author was describing the type of woman who spoke only when spoken to and was basically her husband's slave. That had me worrying, because that's definitely not me.

But the longer I looked at it, and with some help from the most important women in my life, I began to understand the beautiful woman described in this verse. She's worth more than rubies. Rubies are associated with royalty and can be worth more than diamonds.

This woman is more valuable than precious jewels. Not just this woman—but *you*! You're worth more than you could ever imagine. You're a businesswoman, a nurse when your children are sick, a cook, a maid, a partner to your husband, and so much more. You are precious and loved.

I find it humorous that the Bible compares us with jewelry. God knew that's something every woman could understand and relate to!

God put certain women in my life to show me the kind of woman, mother, and wife I should be. One of those women was my Mamaw. In the early 1990s my grandfather suffered a massive stroke that left him partially paralyzed and greatly decreased his ability to communicate with words. My grandmother immediately became his caregiver—the best caregiver imaginable. No doctor or nurse or nursing home could have taken better care of him.

She never complains. Each day when she awakens, she knows her job is to care for him. She's the picture of compassion, kindness, and tenderness, and that makes her one of the most beautiful women I know. I hold these lessons of a truly committed wife close to my heart and cherish them.

Another very important woman in my life is my Meme. I'm very much like her. In fact, if Prov. 31 was about being quiet and subdued, my Meme and I would be in trouble! She's strong, and she can take charge in any situation and make things happen. However, she's never harsh. Everything she does shows Christ's love.

My grandfather has been a preacher and then district superintendent in our denomination, and Meme performs the duties that go along with each of those roles with such dignity and grace. She spoiled me rotten when I was growing up—I'm the only granddaughter. She's also a fantastic mother and wife. I pray that I can be half the woman of strength and gentleness that she has so wonderfully shown me and everyone else with whom she comes in contact.

Last but not least is my mom, one of the greatest women I know. She has balanced being a mother, a wife, and a teacher without ever leaving one area lacking. She stayed at home until my brother and I entered school, then resumed her teaching career. She came home and helped us with homework, did the laundry, put supper on the table, and still found time to laugh and play with us before bed.

Mom, like my grandmother, is also a pastor's wife. Somehow, with everything she has on her plate, she still finds time to do all the many tasks expected of a preacher's wife with the right heart attitude. I know I probably wore her out, but she never stopped having patience with me. She, along with my grandmothers, is the virtuous woman Solomon was speaking of. She is so much more than just a wife or a mother or a teacher—she's a woman of God.

Thank you to all the rubies who show people like me who the Prov. 31 woman really is. Although I'm still just a freshman in college and am not a wife or mother yet, I pray that when I am I will be just like each one of you.

Prayer: *Thank you, Father, for sending women into my life who model the kind of woman you have called me to be. Thank you for shaping me into that woman.*

Thought for the Day: Moms can be precious rubies who are making a difference in the lives of their children.

26 A WEDDING IN CANA OF GALILEE

Joyce Williams

A wedding took place at Cana in Galilee.
—John 2:1

Have you ever wondered what it must have been like to be the mother of Jesus? When Mary felt Him curl His tiny fingers around hers, rocked Him to sleep when He was teething, watched Him take His first steps, treated skinned knees, found Him in the temple, cooked His favorite meal—what did she think?

Then there was that first miracle in Cana. What was Mary thinking that day? Cana has always been one of my favorite sites on each of my seven visits to Israel. But March 2006 added an extra bonus.

I believe it was a divine appointment that Gene and I were seated with Abby and John on our flight from New York to Tel Aviv. For months, all of us had been looking forward to our pilgrimage to the Holy Land.

As we flew through the night, Abby and I caught up on recent years. She and her late husband, Wes, had been very involved members of the church Gene pastored for almost 27 years. They had been scheduled to go on a previous tour, but Wes was diagnosed with cancer. The years after losing him had been lonely.

So we were excited to see the sparkle in her eyes. And Gene and I quickly saw why when we met John, whom she had been dating for about a year. There's no doubt that he's a keeper.

Soaring over the Atlantic, Abby and I talked girl-talk. I asked if they had made any future plans, and she said, "Not really."

Jokingly, I said, "You know, we'll be going to Cana. It's absolutely one of my favorite places—and it's a biblical place for weddings!" We both laughed a little, having no idea what the Lord had planned.

Between naps, I reflected on the first marriage in Cana centuries ago. Mary had seemed eager for her Son to begin His ministry. So she seemed to be pushing Him that day. That encourages my perhaps overly involved mother's heart, I must say! Even the mother of our Lord may have had some control issues.

When we arrived in Israel, our guide, Izzy (short for Israel), was great—very knowledgeable and a true sport. Two other pastors' groups and ours shared many of the experiences as we traveled throughout the Holy Land.

When Abby left the table the next morning at breakfast, John told me he was thinking about proposing on Sunday, when we would be in Tiberias by the Sea of Galilee. I thought that sounded very romantic. Later, just as an aside, I asked Izzy if any pilgrims ever got married in Cana. He said, "Sure. And the weddings are legal. There's a very beautiful wedding chapel in Cana."

We arrived in Tiberias late Saturday afternoon and had dinner at our hotel. It was a beautiful, moonlit evening. I was with friends in the lobby when John and Abby came dashing through the front door looking like two teenagers. John said, "Do you remember that question I was going to ask Abby tomorrow?"

I said, "Yes," holding my breath.

"We just took a stroll along the seashore in the moonlight, and I asked her. The walk, the moon, the timing—it was just right!"

I turned to Abby and asked, "What did you say?"

"I said yes!" she replied.

So we danced a little Israeli "jig" of rejoicing right there in the lobby. And I announced their engagement to everyone within hearing distance. Then I asked, "When do you want to get married?"

"Tomorrow—in Cana!" they replied. We had less than 24 hours to plan a wedding!

I immediately shifted into wedding planner mode! Several of our ladies in the lobby caught the excitement too. John found Izzy and told him the plan. Izzy also jumped into full wedding mode.

Since it was after sundown on Saturday (the Jewish Sabbath), we knew the stores would be reopening. Izzy told us where to go, so the "girls" and I swooped up Abby and headed for downtown Tiberias to shop for a wedding dress. What fun!

Abby found a sweet little dress there, and we helped negotiate a very good price. She found a pearl necklace that was just made for the dress but decided she wouldn't get it. So the rest of us connived and schemed, buying the necklace as a wedding gift for Abby.

Even the shop owner got caught up in our excitement. He was a silversmith and had shown us a beautiful goblet he had crafted, offering it to us at a good price. But doing the "girl thing," we stuck with the pearl necklace. As we were leaving, he came to me and handed over a package—the silver goblet! Now Abby and John had a beautiful communion cup for their wedding!

When we got back to the hotel, Izzy and I talked to the chef in the dining room and ordered a wedding cake. Sure enough, it was ready at eight o'clock Sunday morning. Izzy sneaked it onto our bus, and we headed for Nazareth.

After our tour of Nazareth, John and Abby went shopping for wedding rings. As always, Izzy was right there, helping to find just the right thing. Our entire group was filled with excitement as we boarded the buses and headed out. We followed the curving road our Lord had taken to a wedding in Cana.

It was a gorgeous day. Abby glowed in her wedding dress and her pearl necklace. Although their children could not be there for their wedding, our group became the wedding party "entourage." Those two buses filled with "wedding attendants" just kind of floated along the road.

We gathered in the quaint chapel, and Gene officiated at the wedding. Other couples renewed their wedding vows. There weren't many dry eyes.

We celebrated with the newlyweds as our bus rolled throughout the day. When we stopped for lunch in the Valley of Megiddo, Izzy brought out the wedding cake. The radiant bride cut the cake, and the joyous groom served it to us. What a delightful time!

Mr. and Mrs. John McDonald shared their early honeymoon days with about 60 of us as we completed our pilgrimage. It was such fun to see them so happy together. Their joy splashed over onto each of us.

The miracle of marriage, one of our Father's best plans, delighted our hearts in a new and refreshing way. I thought of how Mary's motherly heart must have been warmed centuries ago when her Son turned the water into wine—thus beginning His earthly ministry. I could just picture her hugging herself and smiling over the fulfillment of the promises she had kept deep within and pondered over the years.

And I believe Jesus may have smiled along with his mother—and with us— as we celebrated another wedding in Cana of Galilee!

Prayer: *Thank you, Lord, for today's miracles.*

Thought for the Day: We never know what wonderful surprises God has in store for us around life's curves.

27 MY ANCHOR HOLDS

Cindy Lipscomb

We have this hope as an anchor for the soul, firm and secure.
—Heb. 6:19

My three daughters, my mother, my friends, and I had enjoyed a fun-filled spring break vacation in Chicago. It had been fun to shop at American Girl Place and take in other wonderful events. As we boarded the Amtrak train to return home on March 15, 1999, our family had no idea that the greatest tragedy of our lives was about to take place.

My husband, Mat, and I had been blessed with three beautiful daughters. They were the joys of our lives. On that fatal day, our daughters—Rainey, 10; Lacey, 8; and 5-year-old Jesse Anne—were having a ball.

Rainey and Lacey were having a slumber party in one of the front sleeper cars with my friend June and her girls, Ashley and Jessica, while my mother, Sudie Davis, Jesse Anne, and I shared a sleeper near the back of the train. It's likely our two precious girls never really knew that our train hit a flatbed truck crossing the tracks about 50 miles south of Chicago. It was a horrific crash. In addition to our two daughters, June and Jessica and seven others were killed, and more than 100 were injured.

The indescribable images were like scenes from the worst possible horror movie. When I was told Rainey and Lacey were gone, it was like a terrible nightmare from which I would soon awaken. One of the hardest moments of my life was calling Mat to tell him about our girls.

The next few days were times of reaching to the very heart of our faith in God. That is what sustained Mat, Jesse Anne, and me through the unimaginable pain of the double funeral service and the two empty bedrooms in our home.

Family, friends, our church family, and even strangers constantly supported us with their prayers and presence. It was amazing to experience the inexpressible caring and concern that poured out over us.

More than anything, we drew courage and comfort from our Heavenly Father. The promises we had claimed throughout our lives sustained us in supernatural ways.

During those days I reflected on those years with our girls. Mat and I had met through the singles group at our church. After our wedding, I enjoyed my lucrative job in retail, constantly advancing up the corporate ladder. Ultimately I was making a six-figure income as a top executive with a major department store. I enjoyed traveling around the world and working 50-60 hours a week. I loved my job.

However, when I became a mother, it was no problem for me to trade it all in. So I gave it up at the age of 34. I always felt that being a stay-at-home mom was my highest calling. My girls, Mat, and my faith in God were truly my life.

After the accident, our lives were so obviously changed. We were grateful God had spared our precious Jesse Anne. Still, there were many times I felt like staying home and crying all day. We knew we had a choice. Through the grace of God and support of so many, we chose to keep going. It's amazing to see how God continues to reward our faith and compensate for our incredible losses.

Not long after the accident, we began to realize that Jesse Anne has been blessed with a beautiful singing voice. As she explored her talents, she auditioned at Germantown (Tennessee) Community Theatre and was cast as Molly in a production of *Annie Warbucks*.

Because of the distance involved, several friends and I decided to begin a theater in DeSoto County, Mississippi. Hence, Desoto Youth Theatre—now DeSoto Family Theatre—was started in 2000 in Southhaven, Mississippi. The mission statement explains the theater's commitment to providing high-quality, family-friendly entertainment that reflects family values. What a blessing the theater has been and continues to be!

I look at the theater as a ministry opportunity and love working with the children. It's a joy to watch them grow and gain confidence. I also enjoy volunteering in a number of other ventures. I feel that the Lord has blessed me, and I want to give back to Him and to our community. Our family's focus continues to be faith, family, and friends.

Oh, yes—there are definitely still days when my heart

aches for Rainey and Lacey. I wonder how they would have matured, what they would be doing, and how they would look if they had survived. But I take comfort in knowing they're in heaven and that one glorious day I'll see them again. I give thanks to Him for that blessed assurance. The rock-solid foundation of my faith in the Lord is my most valued possession, and without it life means nothing. The Rock of my salvation is the anchor of hope for my life.

Prayer: *Thank you, Father, for your sustaining grace through life's greatest tragedies.*

Thought for the Day: When we stay firmly attached to the Rock of our salvation, we'll be safe and secure through the storms of life.

28 GIVE GOD A CHANCE

Stephanie Dawn London

Peace I leave with you; my peace I give you. I do not give to you
as the world gives. Do not let your hearts be troubled
and do not be afraid.
—John 14:27

March 22, 2003, was a beautiful spring day in New York City. I crawled out of my kitchen window and headed up the fire escape to take in the beautiful view of the bay and the Statue of Liberty as the salty ocean breeze drifted over me.

I was planning to call my mom and my sister before spending time reading my Bible. However, my plans were soon abruptly interrupted. About three ladder rungs from the rooftop, my hand slipped. There was nothing I could do as I fell backward over the railing, plummeting five stories to the ground.

On my way up, I had walked past the fifth floor kitchen window of my neighbor Mike, and I said hi to him. So just moments later when he heard something, he knew I had fallen. He grabbed his cell phone and called 911 as he ran down the stairs and around the building to get to me. When he got there, he found two locked wooden fences. He climbed over and yelled, "Steph!" When he heard me call his name, he knew I was still alive.

When Mike finally reached me, I was sitting up and conscious. Having previously trained as a volunteer firefighter, he recognized that miraculously I had no serious brain or spinal injury. He didn't try to comfort me by telling me that help was on the way or that everything would be OK. Instead, we prayed together, ushering me straight to the throne of our Mighty Physician.

After the ambulance came and whisked me away, Mike and a police officer headed up to my apartment looking for a way to contact my parents in Wichita, Kansas. Just then the phone rang. The officer picked it up and said, "Hello. Who is this?" It was my mother calling from Kansas!

"Who is *this*?" she responded, wondering why a man was answering my phone on a Saturday morning. To Mom's horror, the officer told her about the accident. He was not sure of my injuries but was able to assure her that I was conscious and on the way to the hospital.

Mom's strong, calm faith immediately kicked in. She called Dad. He rushed home and called to get flight reservations, but they couldn't get a flight out until noon the next day.

In the meantime, I woke up in intensive care in a dark haze. People were scurrying about. I knew I had been seriously injured, but I was consumed with peace. Everything was in God's hands, so I closed my eyes and fell back into a dazed sleep.

Sometime later I awoke to a doctor hovering over my face as

he talked to Mike. It was so heartwarming when Mike told me he had spoken to my mom. She was being updated on everything that was going on, and I knew she would come as soon as she could to comfort and care for me. Even when we're grown, there's something precious about our mother's touch. We never outgrow wanting our moms when we're hurt or sick. Once again I slipped off into my morphine-induced haze.

The next time I awoke, it was to a startling conversation that I'll never forget. A doctor approached my bed and shoved a clipboard and pen into my hand. He said, "Ms. London, I need you to sign this saying it's OK for me to take your eye out if we get in there and find that there's really nothing there." For just a moment, time stood still. He repeated himself, but I had heard him the first time.

My body began to go into shock, because I had not yet been told about the extent of my injuries.

"What do you mean, if there's nothing there?" I tried to concentrate, gasping for breath. It took all my strength to hold myself together and comprehend what he was saying.

"'If it's not there'—what do you mean? Where did it go?" My spirit cried out, *Give God a chance to heal it!* I didn't want them to take my eye out until God had a chance to do His healing work.

The doctor was explaining that if I did not sign the papers and there was nothing there, it would mean another surgery to clean it out. But my heart just kept saying, *Give God a chance!* I've never experienced such an internal struggle. I knew God could fix things doctors thought were irreparable.

I desperately clung to the promises and faithfulness of Almighty God. I knew He could heal me, and I trusted that He would. I had never needed Him like this before. My eye was either there or it wasn't, so I signed the release. As I handed the clipboard back to the doctor, I firmly grabbed his forearm and emphatically said, "I signed this, but I don't want you to take that eye out!" He assured me that as long as there was anything there, he wouldn't. In complete exhaustion I fell asleep again.

Finally Sunday came, and my parents arrived. What a joy to hear Mom's voice as they came down the hall! I was comforted with peace and delight. I remember thanking them for giving Jesus to me. He was everything to me in this time of need, and I was grateful to them for the Christian heritage they had passed on to me.

Mom spent countless hours at my bedside gently stroking my hair with her soft, comforting, loving touch. After almost a week in the hospital, I was taken to the eye clinic, where my mother immediately transformed the examination chair into a recliner with pillows and blankets. Then she proceeded to fan me as though I were an Egyptian queen. She held my hand as the doctors told us that there was no possibility I would ever regain vision in my injured eye.

That evening Mom called her sister Linda to give her an update. Aunt Linda shared Ps. 112:7-8—"He will have no fear of bad news; his heart is steadfast, trusting in the LORD. His heart is secure, he will have no fear."

Mom claimed those promises for me. Day after day, she

comforted me with hope and encouragement, bathing me in her prayers and scripture passages.

Now, several years and many procedures later, I have a great life. Although the retina in my damaged eye is displaced and I have no vision in it, I can rejoice that the eyes of my faith are stronger than ever.

Prayer: *Father, help me be a strong, godly mother who gives my children gentle care and unwavering faith.*

Thought for the Day: A Prov. 31 mother ministers strength, comfort, and faith to her children.

29

FUN
IN THE
FISHBOWL
Gail MacDonald

A cheerful heart is good medicine.
—Prov. 17:22

Children growing up in a pastor's home not only have to cope with the common fears of childhood, but they also often become aware early in life of the many conflicts and problems that require the attention of their father or mother as he or she leads a congregation. In many cases, their joy is in danger. It's often a challenge to maintain a light and cheery attitude in a pastor's home.

As a young mother, I was sensitive to this and came to believe strongly that my role in our home was that of "mood-setter." Fairly or unfairly, my family often caught my moods. If I exuded merriment, the family usually picked it up. If my spirit was somber or grumpy, it wasn't long until other family members were playing back what they saw in me. This caused me to give careful attention to the business of setting the mood.

It began early in the morning when I roused our children to greet the day. Even when they were still in their cribs, I tried to launch their days with a song and a smile. The underlying message was that God's mercies are new every morning.

I was also aware of setting a light and fun mood at mealtimes. If one of the children entered the kitchen grumbling about the menu, I would say, "Uh-oh—you'll need to go out and come back in a second time." And with exaggerated enthusiasm, I would say, "Try coming back like this: 'Oh, boy! Look what Mom's made for supper tonight!'"

When dinner was leftovers, I called the evening "Italy night," and every family member knew what to expect—or not expect. The lights would be dimmed to suggest the ambience of an Italian restaurant. Actually, I simply didn't want anyone to see what he or she was eating. The children caught the humor as long as Italy nights were few and far between.

Crazy things like this usually brought laughter at my silliness. But an insistence on maintaining a light attitude and fun atmosphere in our home paid off.

Now, many years later, our grown children have their own families, and I'm grateful to see they enjoy eating together in the same manner that they were taught during their childhoods. A regular dinner together as a family with conversation that is positive and enjoyable is among the greatest gifts parents can give their children.

In the larger sense, we desired that our children see all of life as a gift. We battled against the notion of entitlement or of taking for granted the blessings of a generous God. Today, more than 40 years later, this mood of gratitude set so early in our children's lives keeps us close as an extended family.

When I was a young mother, I wish I had been more aware of the subtle ways children are expected to "perform" when Dad or Mom is a pastor. I never understood how easy it was for them to feel the sometimes unreasonable pressure of those expectations whether put on them by the congregation, the ministry parents, or even themselves. I can see more clearly now how often they felt an obligation to make the family look good or were unwilling to take any risks that might jeopardize their parents' reputation.

If I had it to do over again, I would work harder to remind our children that they're not expected to be perfect, nor are they responsible for our success. This is a message that needs to be frequently communicated in a pastor's home—or any home for that matter.

I have very few regrets about our family life when I look back to those days when my children were young. The benefits of being part of a pastor's family far outweigh the liabilities. But I'm convinced that the reason I can be so positive about the experience began in the earliest days when I committed to maintaining a mood of lightness, cheerfulness, and gratitude—and that it would begin with me.

Prayer: *Father, help me to make our home a place where my children are always happy to be.*

Thought for the Day: Home should be a place where the hurts of the world are healed.

30

ANNIE'S EYES

Sherri McCready

We live by faith, not by sight.
—2 Cor. 5:7

We were getting ready for church one Sunday morning when suddenly my five-year-old daughter, Annie, collapsed onto the couch, holding her head in obvious agony. My mommy's heart knew from the sound of her cry that her pain was real and frightening.

After a few minutes of sitting with Annie, I decided she needed to see a doctor. Annie's big brother and three-year-old sister, as well as her newborn baby brother, were waiting to leave for church. "What's wrong with Annie, Mommy?" my oldest son asked.

"Annie doesn't feel so great today, so Mommy is going to call the doctor." The rest of the day passed in a blur that included an emergency room visit and a CAT scan that showed nothing abnormal.

The next morning I was awakened by Annie's small hand on my arm: "Mommy, the steps look funny to me." When I opened my eyes and looked into her precious little face, a horrible feeling washed over me. Her eyes didn't look right.

Everything seemed to be going dark for Annie. As the week progressed, her vision grew worse. One afternoon she very calmly asked, "Mommy will you be my eyes?"

We set another appointment for Annie to see our family doctor, and he could immediately see that her optic nerves were swollen. He called to schedule a spinal tap and an MRI.

That evening was our son's seventh birthday party. The house was filled with our family and friends and the happy chaos of a child's party. But there, lost in the middle of it all, was my Annie, her little hand clutching onto my jeans.

Her daddy understood. Shannon bravely swept her to his shoulders and placed a water gun in her hands, "Spray your brother, Annie!" She giggled and fired the water gun with all her heart. I couldn't laugh with her. Instead, I slipped out the door to the side of the house to let out the tears that were crowding my heart.

Throughout the week I saw Jesus in my prayers. He was walking in front of me—turned around and facing me. *Come on. Come on.*

Where are we going? my heart responded. I felt my legs of faith nearly buckle beneath the weight of my pain, but I willed them to move ahead anyway—just like Annie, one step at a time.

Shannon and I sang with Annie all the way to the hospital. I'll never forget the sound of her voice: "I could sing of your love forever," words from her favorite church song. Shannon and I listened as the tears streamed down our faces and we stifled our sobs. We held her hands as we walked into the hospital, and she trusted us wherever we led her.

That day began a journey for our family that would take us down many corridors of faith and an eventual rare diagnosis of multiple sclerosis for Annie. Her vision eventually returned and was replaced by a weakness in her legs that made walking difficult, thus beginning the rollercoaster walk of faith that MS demands. One day, when she was brave enough, she asked me, "Mommy, why did God let me have MS?" Jesus gave me the words to say.

"Annie, is God good or bad?"

"He's good," she said simply.

"Is He big or small?" I asked.

"He's big."

Finally I asked, "Does God love you or hate you?"

She smiled. "He loves me."

Then with my own heart full of faith I said, "Annie, if God is good and big and He loves you, can we trust that He has a good, big, and loving reason for your MS?"

The words went in slowly and deeply, like a piece of steak that needed a lot of chewing but grew more delicious with every bite. She accepted the words and went off to play.

She was a picture of faith. She clung to the ones she trusted. She stayed near our voices. She felt safe and allowed us to be her vision. She seemed to trust that we could see something that she could not while all of us trusted that God could see something we could not. Like the old hymn:

Be thou my vision, O Lord of my heart;
Naught be all else to me, save that Thou art—
Thou my best thought, by day or by night,
Waking or sleeping, Thy presence my light.

And He has been faithful. Although Annie still struggles with her disease, He continues to illuminate our pathway.

Prayer: *Father, thank you for calling me to trust you with all my heart and instructing me to never lean on my own understanding.*

Thought for the Day: Our Good Shepherd leads us in the shadowy valleys when we can't see our way. His love lights our hearts and lives.

PROFIT FROM LOSSES

Jerene Marable

It was good for me to be afflicted
so that I might learn your decrees.
—Ps. 119:71

For 30 years as a businesswoman, I grappled with profits and losses. For the past seven years I've wrestled with profiting *from* losses. I learned the hard way that material gain is a poor substitute for spiritual loss. Fortunately, I've also learned that spiritual gain from material loss is priceless.

I got married the first time when I was just 18. I take full responsibility for my choices, but I also realize that my family of origin set me up for failure. My parents divorced in my early teens, and my mom died when I was 18. We seldom attended church, and God was not a big part of our lives.

Two daughters were born of my marriage, but it ended in divorce after 17 years. In hindsight I realize that the divorce was a big mistake that caused a lot of pain for many people. Although I married a second time without considering God's plan, my second marriage, to Ron, was much better and lasted more than 20 years.

Ron and I worked hard and earned lots of money. We owned interest in 15 nursing homes, sole ownership of three convenience stores, and various real estate holdings. In the process, we worked many seven-day weeks.

We tried to live right and help others, and although our lifestyle was very comfortable, it was never extravagant. However, we rarely prayed and rarely attended church or gave time, thought, or money to God. We were just too busy.

Life changed swiftly and dramatically in March 1996. Like the psalmist, I discovered, "Before I was afflicted, I went astray, but now I obey your word" (Ps. 119:67). My afflictions came through losses in family and finances.

When word came that fateful day that my oldest daughter Leanne was a passenger in a truck that had been struck by a train, I panicked, screamed, and begged God to spare her life. It took us hours to make our way home from Denver to her hospital bed in Little Rock, Arkansas.

While still in a coma, two weeks after her accident, Leanne had corrective surgery because of an attendant's ineptness. I reached my breaking point during the surgery. Suddenly I realized it was time for me to start praying for my own spiritual health and not just for my daughter's physical health.

In a family waiting room in that hospital I turned my life over to Christ. I confessed my sins, released my shame, and experienced God's loving presence and forgiveness. I promised to serve and follow Him the rest of my life. Thank God for the faith that He gave me that night—because things were about to get even worse.

Six weeks to the day after Leanne's accident, we discovered that Ron had multiple myeloma cancer. For the next two years he aggressively battled the cancer. Leanne remained unconscious. My life was consumed with caring for my dying daughter, her two young boys, and my terminally ill husband.

Ron died in August of 1998. At that time I did not think I had any kind of future, much less a hopeful future as promised in Jer. 29:11. I grieved his death deeply for several months until one day I made up my mind that my old life was over and it was time to begin again. With God's help and my faith and several friends who stood by me, I got a fresh start.

Leanne remained in a coma until she died in December 2000. Since I had grieved over her lifeless body for four years, her death was not as hard on me as Ron's had been. I realized it was her time to die and that she was in a much better place. Again, my faith in God sustained me and healed my wounds. God graciously ministered to me as He helped me release all of my regrets concerning Leanne's life and death.

Because of some poor decisions by Ron and some unfair treatment by his business partner, I lost my portion of ownership in eight nursing homes as well as much of my real estate holdings. I am not impoverished, but I have lost a large portion of my financial security because of dishonesty, betrayal, and circumstances beyond my control.

But God has been faithful. I've learned much and profited greatly from my losses. I've learned to forgive. As I repeatedly read Ps. 37 for an entire year, God gradually helped me let go of my hurt. I have no ill will toward the young man who caused my daughter's death, and I have forgiven those who betrayed me in our businesses.

Although recent years have brought more challenges and losses, I'm learning more about prayer. My afflictions have motivated me to cry out to God and have strengthened my faith. I've spent many hours and days talking to the Lord. He has heard and answered my prayers. Through my faith in God I have found internal peace despite external circumstances.

Each day I thank God for the opportunity to serve Him. It has been my privilege to be a part of mission trips to ten different countries. I'm looking forward to the exciting future that I believe God has planned for me. I want to pass along the faith that God has established within me. By God's grace I intend to profit from my losses.

Prayer: *Thank you, Lord, for turning losses to gains.*

Thought for the Day: Our Father brings good from all things.

THE UNBROKEN CIRCLE

Paula Martin

32

*Do not forget the things your eyes have seen or let them slip
from your heart as long as you live. Teach them to
your children and to their children after them.*
—Deut. 4:9

Mothers have such an impact on our lives. My husband, Jerry, and I are blessed to have godly mothers and grandmothers and are very grateful for that shared heritage. It's awesome to realize that a mother's faith extends beyond this world. That truth was tangibly manifested in our family recently at the homegoing of our family patriarch, my father-in-law, Bill Martin Sr.

Bill had always been a strong, God-fearing leader who had learned at his mother's knee how to live for Jesus. She had taught him well, and he had carefully shared this great legacy with his extended family and many friends to the end of his life. His most fervent prayer echoed his beloved mother's desire that there would be an unbroken circle of the entire family in heaven some day.

Bill fell a few months before his death. In the hospital he

was diagnosed with pneumonia. The family gathered around him. His strong constitution and desire to be with his family revived him. In a rehabilitation facility he appeared to be getting a little better until an infection put him back in the hospital several more times. Confusion and severe pain set in on this man who had always had a brilliant mind.

It was difficult for the family members to see him slipping away both in mind and body. He was surrounded by his family in the hospital during his last few days and was greatly comforted to have all four children and Wanda, his beloved wife of nearly 66 years, holding his hand around the clock.

There were precious times of prayer, singing hymns, and reminiscing about the good old days, even through our tears. Finally, however, Bill's pain became so severe that none of us wanted to keep him here if God was calling him home.

About 30 minutes before he passed away, he looked up toward heaven and said with eyes wide open, "Mother, I'm coming home!" Then a little later, he said just one more word, "Bye," as he quietly slipped away to be with his Lord, his beloved mother and spiritual mentor, as well as other family members. We felt sure she heard those glorious words and eagerly awaited his homecoming.

Bill's one request was that Jerry, one who knew and loved him best, would deliver the funeral message. He knew Jerry had delivered quite a few funeral messages, including his own grandmother's.

Jerry kept saying he really didn't know if he could do it. However, after speaking with his mother, who reiterated Bill's wishes, Jerry decided to trust God to give him the strength to carry out that monumental assignment. It was amazing to see how the Lord used our grandchildren to help "Poppy" accomplish this.

The youngest, three-year-old Blake, wanted to spend the night with his Poppy the night Bill passed away. In the morning when we woke up with Blake sleeping in the middle, he climbed on top of Jerry and asked, "Did Grandpa Bill go to heaven?" Jerry assured Blake that he was in heaven with Jesus and his parents. Blake hugged his Poppy, sensing his need for comfort.

Then Blake said, "No, Grandpa Bill isn't in heaven. He's at church walking up and down the aisles with Jesus!" Blake had just seen the Easter drama at our church called "Living Pictures." He had watched a man portraying Jesus walking the aisles with many people following him. Jerry tried to explain to Blake that he was walking with Jesus now and was really in "Big Church—heaven," not just "Little Church" here on earth. Jerry whispered to me, "And a little child will lead them."

On the day of the funeral, our oldest grandchild, Lauren, a very smart and sympathetic 11-year-old, asked if she could ride with Poppy ahead of the rest of the family. They had a special time together as he drove to the church. Then, before they got out of the car, Lauren asked her Poppy if she could pray for him, that Jesus would give him strength for this task. And she did.

The other five grandchildren soon came to their Poppy's side as they gazed at Grandpa Bill's body in the casket at the church. They, too, sensed Poppy's deep need for comfort and strength. They offered their small hands and big hearts to him as they gathered around to slip handwritten notes into the casket and say their final goodbyes.

Jerry delivered a touching message. Many family members also spoke lovingly of their relationship with this great and godly man. It was especially touching to hear the tributes shared by the great-grandchildren. Even in their young hearts, they realized that their beloved great-grandpa, the man who said, "Mother, I'm coming home," had finally made it to heaven.

As I reflect on my beloved father-in-law's life and desires, I see a great need for all of us to pray for this unbroken circle tradition to carry on through many generations. Thus, Bill's final wish of seeing his family around the throne in an unbroken circle will be fulfilled.

My greatest prayer is that my children and all their progeny would someday join me in heaven. The ultimate compliment would be for them to say, "Mother, I'm coming home." And our circle, too, will be unbroken.

Prayer: *Father, help me be a mother who sparks heavenly aspirations in the hearts, lives, and souls of my loved ones.*

Thought for the Day: The greatest gift we can give our children is a hunger for things that will outlast this world.

33 CRUMBS OF FAITH

Joyce Williams

*"Oh, woman, your faith is something else! What you want is
what you get!" Right then her daughter became well.*
—Matt. 15:28, TM

Sometimes when our kids—regardless of their ages—are
in times of illness, distress, or need, I must confess that my faith
is stretched. Between us, Gene and I have 7 children, 14
grandchildren, 5 great-grands—with more of those coming
down the pike! And they live in five different states. So there
are times when we seem to be consumed with their problems and troubles. The miles separating us make those situations more difficult. I find myself turning to the Word for role
models to strengthen my faith. One of my favorites is found in
Matt. 15.

We don't even know her name. She was a despised Gen-
tile—a heathen infidel—considered on a good day to have
the social standing of a dog. Yet this story of the Syro-Phoeni-
cian mother is a great example of grace and tolerance.

Her daughter was demon-possessed. I can't imagine the
horrors this poor mother and daughter encountered every

day. Don't you wonder what the other women in town said about them? It's very possible they speculated about what this distressed mother had done to deserve a daughter who was so desperately tormented. Yet when she heard that Jesus, the great miracle-worker, was traveling through her area, she determined to seek Him out and implore Him to heal her daughter.

When she approached Jesus, I'm sure everyone was astonished at her audacity. How dare she presume that Jesus, a Jew, would listen to a person of her descent! It's also amazing that with her background she exhibited such faith in Jesus as Savior.

When she approached the Lord, she humbly acknowledged her sinful unworthiness. Then she cried out, "Have mercy on me, Lord, Son of David! My daughter is suffering terribly from demon-possession" (v. 22).

No one was surprised when Jesus at first appeared to ignore her—not answering a word (v. 23). I can relate. Some of my prayers for our children have seemed to bounce off the ceiling and boomerang back onto my head! Then the disciples tried to send her away because she kept crying out, making a scene.

I'm sure her heart fell when Jesus responded, "I was sent only to the lost sheep of Israel" (v. 24). But she still didn't give up. She continued interceding, kneeling before Jesus and simply imploring, "Lord, help me" (v. 25).

Jesus again appeared to deny her request, sounding somewhat harsh when he said, "It is not right to take the children's bread and toss it to their dogs" (v. 26). This "bread" Jesus referred to is His grace, and the children represented true believers in Israel. Jesus was testing the woman's faith and perseverance.

She passed the test—she still didn't give up. Oh, how I need to learn from her example! She replied to our Lord and Savior, "Even the dogs eat the crumbs that fall from their masters' table" (v. 27). All she asked was that a crumb might fall her way in spite of her background. She was not offended by Jesus' comments or apparent lack of response. Because she believed, she persevered.

How I cherish Jesus' answer! "'Woman you have great faith! Your request is granted.' And her daughter was healed from that very hour" (v. 28).

That's what I desire—great faith. When our prayers for our children seem to encounter an impenetrable wall, even a crumb of faith can hold us steady. After all, our Father has a history of bringing down walls. The key for us is to continue to believe that our Good Shepherd will do what He says He will do.

Someday, when we're together in heaven, I want to meet that mother and daughter. I'll finally know their names. I want to personally thank that persistent prayer warrior for the example of her faith and endurance.

And perhaps we'll share crumbs of heavenly manna as we sit at our Lord's feet.

Prayer: *Dear Good Shepherd, please increase my faith. May I trust you to care for my children and loved ones, regardless of how many miles separate us.*

Thought for the Day: Perseverance in prayer always brings an answer. Sometimes God's answer is *yes,* sometimes *no,* sometimes *wait.* The key is to trust His response.

34 UNEXPLAINED PEACE

Regina Robinson

Being confident of this, that he who began a good work in you
will carry it on to completion until the day of Christ Jesus.
—Phil. 1:6

The day before Valentine's Day proved to be the most difficult 24 hours my husband and I had ever endured. We had been eagerly anticipating the 20-week ultrasound appointment that would tell us the gender and health of our second child.

As we entered the appointment with the radiologist, our 10-month-old daughter, Jordyn, was unusually calm, which we appreciated. The radiologist entered the room, chatted, and began the examination. After only a few minutes of observation, he quickly interrupted our casual conversation with seven life-changing words, "There is something wrong with the baby!"

Our hearts were gripped with concern as he continued to show us the baby's brain and explained that there was too much fluid, which suppressed the brain tissue. The condition is called hydrocephalus, and it could delay normal development. He shared his opinion of the high likelihood that the baby might not survive and that if he or she did, the baby could have a poor quality of life. He concluded by saying that we needed to terminate the pregnancy.

What a blow! Something was wrong, and our baby could die? We were numb and confused. He brought in another specialist to confirm what he saw, and she agreed with him. As he concluded the testing, he had not yet told us the gender of our baby. After Jua asked him, he said that it was a boy. How precious! Even under the circumstances, we were having a son, and we knew that we would not terminate his life.

As I watched the tears trickle down my husband's face, I wondered if those were tears of happiness or sadness. I was filled with despair as we gathered our things and walked out of the office. We rode separately, because Jua was in and out of pastoral meetings and I was going home for Jordyn's nap. As I drove away, my tears freely flowed, as I began to feel the anguish of our situation.

I cried for Jua. Having been raised by his mom in a single-parent home, he had not been fortunate to have godly parents—particularly a dad—to teach him about biblical manhood. As a college student, he accepted Christ and was blessed to have godly male peer influences and then discipleship by Campus Crusade for Christ male staff. God gave him a burden and desire to raise his own children, especially sons, in a biblically affirming manner, and I wanted that for him. I cried for the loss of that dream in the way I thought that dream would look for our family.

I cried for Jordyn and the changes to her childhood in

helping to raise a sibling with special needs. She was a sweet girl with a kind demeanor to all who interacted with her. Would her personality change or be shaped due to more attention being placed on her little brother, who would need so much intervention?

I cried for myself and the fact that I did not know if I possessed the extraordinary patience this kind of parenting would require. What did God intend to do with our situation? I felt an immense weight in my heart due to fear of the known and the unknown, and it ached with the loss of my own personal dream.

From that appointment came several more sessions with specialists, radiologists, and pediatricians, who confirmed our worst fears. We had more tests run that also confirmed our baby boy had Down syndrome in addition to the hydrocephalus, and my mind once again was filled with questions. Up to this point, I have not faced threatening circumstances that shook me to the core. I guess it was time for a shakedown! God took me through weeks of praise, prayer, anguish, anxiety, doubt, guilt, and yet I've tried to remain steadfast in His love for me.

I have yet to know what he intends to do with our family and our little boy, whom we named Josiah. "Josiah" means *The Lord supports*. As we prayed about his name, I read definitions and synonyms that better explain the meaning of the word "support" to confirm the understanding of what our Lord is doing with our precious son.

Support—*to carry all or part of the weight of; to keep from falling or sinking; to give strength to.* Synonyms are *bear, hold up, sustain, strengthen, reinforce, stand by; (noun) help, foundation, beam, sustenance, assistance, aid.*

I have realized that the Lord is our foundation and our rock, no matter what obstacles appear in our path. Although I'm unsure of what the future holds for our family—whether a miracle of some sort will occur, we will have unbelievably hard trials with our Josiah—one thing I do know is that the Lord has not forgotten us. He has not forsaken His promise of peace for us, and He is not finished His work within us. The day of that first appointment, Jua read Philippians 1:6 in his quiet time.

I do not always feel confident, but I know the foundation of my confidence, and I will rest in knowing the promise the Lord supports.

Prayer: *Thank you, Father, for your peace that surpasses my human understanding.*

Thought for the Day: There's great hope when we lean on His everlasting arms.

35  WHAT'S IN A NAME?

Cheryl Roland

*Fear not, for I have redeemed you; I have called
you by name; you are mine.*
—Isa. 43:1

Little Bradley faithfully knelt at his bedside and prayed for a baby brother, confident that God would hear and answer his prayer. It was difficult to break the news, but the parents were sure Bradley would understand and adjust. "Bradley," his dad explained, "the doctor said you are going to have a little sister!"

Full of faith and determination, Bradley questioned repeatedly, night after night. "Dad, just in case it's a boy, what would we name him?" "Mom, just in case it's a boy, what would we name him?" Much to everyone's surprise, a bouncing baby boy was born, and they named him Justin Case.

What decision could be more defining than the names we give our babies? My enthusiastic opinions tumbled out before I could catch them. "Our first grandbaby should have a Bible name, a name that depicts strength, faith, and leadership." Family members chimed in to make suggestions. Even strangers felt free to ask about the name and then expressed their likes and dislikes. We heard noble names, pet names, peculiar names, nicknames, and family names. We bought books of names and researched the Internet for names. We were careful to watch for spelling preferences and the way three names sounded together. We also had to take into consideration the initials and what they might spell. How could the name be twisted to mean something else that would damage our little guy for a lifetime? This was a major decision that required prayerful thought. Little did we know the baby would change everyone's name.

When I first heard it, I could hardly believe my ears. Did our little grandbaby, Bryce Andrew, call me by name? Did Bryce really say *Grammy?* No, it sounded more like *Bammy* or *Mammy.* Whatever it was, I couldn't have been happier! I wrote down the date he spoke and then proceeded to call all the family to report that Bryce knew me by name.

What's in a name? Are names important to God? One of the first responsibilities given to Adam was to name the animals: "Now the LORD God had formed out of the ground all the beasts of the field and all the birds of the air. He brought them to the man to see what he would name them; and whatever the man called each living creature, that was its name" (Gen. 2:19). Amazingly, Eve had not been created, so Adam had to rely on his own imagination. Scholars say that in the ancient world, to give a person a name was a sign of authority over him or her. By naming the animals, Adam declared dominion or power over them.

As with Adam, our Heavenly Father calls us by name. He speaks words of comfort and authority over us throughout the Scriptures. Isaiah 43:1 is one example. To think that our Heavenly Father—our Creator—not only redeems us but also calls us by our names!

We in turn reveal our submission to God and His authority over us when we recognize His name as holy. Jesus taught His disciples to pray, "Our Father . . . hallowed be your name . . . on earth as it is in heaven" (Matt. 6:9-10).

Oh, the joy that Jesus Christ must experience when we teach our babies that God has a name! God's name is holy. At every stage of their maturity, we must pray that the name of God takes on new meaning; *Father, Jesus, Lord, Friend, Savior, Sanctifier, Comforter, Counselor, Almighty God, the Prince of Peace,* the great *I AM.* "Everyone who calls on the name of the Lord will be saved" (Rom. 10:13).

Careless expressions that incorporate God's name as a statement of surprise, upset, delight, or disgust break the heart of God. Titles that belong to God alone, when misused are an infringement on the rights of God.

Just in case we miss the significance of keeping God's name holy, He has recorded in Exod. 20—the 10 Commandments —the foundations of our faith, that His name is to be reverenced. He is worthy of our highest praise and deepest respect. Philippians 2:9 says, "God exalted Him to the highest place and gave him the name that is above every name, that at the name of Jesus every knee should bow, in heaven and on earth and under the earth, and every tongue confess that Jesus Christ is Lord, to the glory of God the Father."

Ah, did you just hear your baby speak the name of Jesus? Write down the date and call all the family to celebrate!

Prayer: *Heavenly Father, may I listen when you call me by name. And may I always answer and respond in accordance with your plans for me.*

Thought for the Day: Jesus is the name above all names.

36 OUTLAWS' MOM

Kim Singson

I tell you: Love your enemies and pray for those who persecute you.
—Matt. 5:44

I serve as district superintendent of the North East India District of the Church of the Nazarene.

I was awakened late one night shortly after my husband's death to find men with guns—outlaws—surrounding my home in Manipur, India. My momentary panic was replaced by peace, knowing that Jesus was with me. I began to pray for these men, referring to them as my sons.

As they hovered outside, the Holy Spirit began to penetrate their hearts. When dawn began to break, I went out to meet them, saying, "Good morning, sons." They lowered their guns. I said I had been praying for them throughout the night. Then I told them about Jesus. Several of the outlaws began to weep, crying as they confessed their sins. The others turned away, leaving us unharmed.

Five days later, some of the men attended my church. They soon began to call me *Mom*. I counseled and discipled my new *sons* for months. I was amazed when they started tithing. Eventually, several became a vital part of our churches and continue to support our ministry.

Two of these former outlaws are now at the seminary, studying to be pastors. Although these men were once my enemies, today I count them among my closest friends. They tell me, "Mom, whenever you need help, you tell us. We will help you. We will not let anyone harm you."

Note from Joyce:

Kim was dedicated to the Lord's service by her mother and grandfather when she was only a few days old. She made the decision to follow Christ when she was nine, and she accepted God's call into fulltime Christian ministry as a young teenager.

After graduating from a Christian high school, Kim attended a university. She began teaching, and she organized the Ladies' Gospel Team to share Christ through Manipur, India.

She met and fell in love with the principal of the school where she taught, Rev. T. S. Singson, and they were married. They shared their mutual call of spreading the gospel in northern India for seven years.

Shortly after T. S. passed away in 2001, Kim accepted the assignment to oversee 17 churches. Although grieving the loss of her dear husband, Kim was confident that she was following God's plan for her life.

Throughout the years, Kim has faithfully climbed the hills of Manipur and blazed trails everywhere she goes. Because she's a woman, it's not always been easy to gain the acceptance of her people.

Her four children call her blessed, and she is the caregiver to her aging parents as well. The Lord faithfully provides the strength she needs, and she is rewarded by seeing her children following her path.

The sons she speaks of, together with some of the area's political leaders, government officials, and wealthy individuals, faithfully support Pastor Kim's ministry.

Prayer: *Father, please help me minister faithfully and fearlessly wherever you place me.*

Thought for the Day: "'Don't be afraid,' the prophet answered. 'Those who are with us are more than those who are with them'" (2 Kings 6:16).

37

MY MOTHER, MY FRIEND

Kathryn Sipper

No one knows about that day or hour, not even the angels
in heaven, nor the Son, but only the Father.
—Matt. 24:36

My wedding day promised to be everything I had hoped: blue skies, sunny, warm. I was filled with an expectancy I had never experienced. In those last few moments of waiting, I had time to reflect on a similar morning about five years earlier. That morning—like this one—was about to change my life forever.

The organ began the familiar wedding march, and I started down the aisle with Dad on one arm and Mom on the other. I had wanted my mom to be part of this special day, because I wanted to show God and the world just how important my mother was to me, that I loved her and that I wanted to honor her part in my life. I stood there remembering the promises I made to God that other morning almost five years earlier.

My memories are so clear, as if it were yesterday. It was the end of summer in New Jersey. The only thing unusual about it was that I slept through the alarm clock and woke up late—almost one hour to the minute. The train I usually took was pulling out about the time I was wiping the sleep from my eyes.

On my way out the door, an hour late, I was thinking about the day ahead. It was Tuesday, September 11, 2001, and I was in the last two weeks of my position with a large financial services company in New York City. I had resigned only a few days earlier after accepting an offer with another company based in New Jersey.

That was the day we have come to know as 9/11. My company had offices in midtown Manhattan and at the World Trade Centers. In fact, my group had reorganized, and I was added to an existing team in 5 World Trade, known as Tower 5. I was supposed to have relocated during the summer of 2001, but some internal decisions had postponed the move. So my office was still midtown.

Many miracles happened that day. Some call it a series of coincidences that allowed me to travel in and out of the city, to be in the middle of chaos, and get home by train four-and-a-half hours after leaving for work. But I know otherwise. It was all part of God's plan. I survived for His purpose.

The most startling part for me was that I was in the middle of world-changing events, yet I had very little realization of what was unfolding. In fact, I kept trying to get to work.

From the commuter train I was on, I saw images in the distance of burning smoke coming from the Towers. How could that happen—a plane hitting a building? Did the pilot have a heart attack? Why weren't trains running to lower Manhattan? Why was my cell phone dead? Did I forget to pay my bill?

I kept moving as if everything were normal, not comprehending the signs of the horrible tragedy unfolding at the World Trade Center, at the Pentagon, and in Pennsylvania.

Finally I saw a CNN broadcast at a newsstand in Penn Station. This was serious. I knew I had to get out of there. It seemed certain we were going to war, and I didn't want to be stuck there. I wanted to go home and see my family again.

As the rest of the country began shutting down, a train to New Jersey was announced. Our departure was delayed, but we were finally released to go through the tunnel. I saw a chilling image in the distance: a black column of smoke from ground to sky as a tower fell. At the Newark station officials with hardhats and megaphones gave directions to the crowd. It didn't matter when random trains pulled in or where they were going, as long as they continued to arrive and the destination was away from New York.

That day, when it felt as if my life were in the balance, I saw myself standing before the Lord, reviewing my life. In those moments of reflection, I realized how much it was all about me. I could see that my priorities were skewed and asked myself where God really fit into my life. I breathed three short, sincere prayers.

God, forgive me for my sins. I realized how little I had invested in the people God had placed in my life. There was always a good reason—excuse after excuse.

Father, please protect the people I love. I knew in those moments that if I lost my life I would die without having done anything to pass on the renewed love and grace God had given me that day. If I survived, I knew the focus of my life would change. It was time for restoration.

With deep sadness, I recognized that I had built a wall of bitterness between me and my mother. I had unfairly blamed her for the issues in my life. Whose fault was it that I felt I hardly knew her? What had I done about removing that barrier? What if I never saw her again?

I could feel God speaking to me about forgiveness. Christ made himself a willing sacrifice for my sins, fulfilled His purpose, and made my salvation possible. He had forgiven me completely, and to be like Him, I must forgive. I relinquished my life issues to Him permanently.

Father, forgive me for not fulfilling your plan for me. Help me to find my purpose.

These God-driven discoveries shed a new light on Christ's ministry of forgiveness and reconciliation. In the time I have on earth, I want to pass on Christ's legacy of love to those around me.

My mom called me that night and said, "I thank God we don't mourn today but can celebrate and be thankful for who is still with us." My mother was talking about *me*! I felt the walls tumbling down.

Five years later, as I walked down the aisle to meet my groom, I smiled tearfully at my mother, my friend.

Prayer: *Lord, thank you for life-defining moments that show me how you want me to live. Give me strength to fulfill your purpose for my life.*

Thought for the Day: Because Jesus forgives unconditionally, so can I.

38

A RARE COLLECTION

Hope Tallent

Many women do noble things, but you surpass them all.
—Prov. 31:29

I have a rare, if not unheard of, hobby. Some comb the seashore for hours looking for the perfect shell to add to their collection. Others travel far and wide to attain exotic coins or stamps. My travels have brought me an entirely unique collection. I collect moms.

I didn't realize this truth until recently as I was assessing my extraordinarily privileged existence and God's providence in it. My compilation naturally began in college, as those years were my first living away from home.

While Jean is entirely too young to actually be my mother, she was the first lady to step into that role for me. Jean's advice to me was always dispensed with great concern for me. Her encouragement and genuine smile etched out a place for her in my heart.

One tip she shared with me is one I remember every day as I prepare to face the world: "Always wear lipstick. It helps you put your best face forward." To this day, I'm rarely without lipstick!

When I graduated from college, I moved with my sister, Heather, to South Korea to work as an English teacher. God arranged for my next mom to appear just days after we arrived. Cathy's model of leadership and Southern hospitality was just what I needed. She and her husband had moved from Oklahoma, leaving their two grown sons behind. There were times Cathy and her husband needed us as much as we needed them.

Cathy is a go-getter. She loved opening her home on Friday and Saturday nights to anyone—Korean or otherwise—who cared to join them. She had a knack for turning an evening playing games and eating popcorn into a real event. She thrived on activity, whether it was an American-style picnic with Korean students featuring tuna fish sandwiches and potato chips or an evening at a Korean singing room with silly people singing "Dancing Queen" or "MMMBop!"

One day I mentioned to Cathy that it would be fun to have a bonfire and make s'mores. The next weekend we enjoyed not only a bonfire with s'mores but also a hayride with camp songs, all organized by Cathy! The first snow of the year fell that night, but it did not ruin the fun. Cathy's examples of love, friendship, acceptance, hospitality, compassion, joy, and adventure are what I appreciate most about her.

I became acquainted with my next mom the year I lived in Kenya as a volunteer at Africa Nazarene University. I guess you can get farther away from Kansas than Kenya, but it didn't seem like it at the time. It was during the year in Kenya that I was encouraged and comforted by my adopted mom, Julie.

Julie was a missionary with grown daughters back in Tennessee and Kentucky. I met her my first day on campus. The first thing she said to me was mixed with excitement and homesickness. "You look just like my Erin! Both of you are tall with gorgeous blonde hair." I'm merely quoting here—I did not make up these words. But her flattery won me over, and we formed a strong bond that grew stronger with time.

Julie and I shared love, laughs, carrot cake, and tears. But most of all, we shared life—the ins and outs as well as the ups and downs. I'm so thankful to have been provided with such a resource of insight and strength—not to mention that she was the best shopping teacher ever! She could out-bargain even the greatest of spend-thrifts. Here is the rule in Kenyan markets: "Ask for a quarter of their first price, and never pay more than half of it. Do not feel bad if you walk away feeling that you practically stole your purchase. They would not have sold it to you if they did not make a profit." I saved many a shilling under her excellent tutelage.

I also adopted the mom of my best friend in Kenya. It seemed natural that Kendi, who became my sister there, would let me share her mom, Christine—Mama Kendi. It is customary in Kenya to refer to mothers by using their first-born's name. Mama Kendi helped keep a roof over my head and a pillow under it when I needed a place to stay in Nairobi. Her chapatti, mtoke, iriyo, and pilau helped keep meat on my bones too. Because of Christine's kindness, I truly felt like part of the family.

In no way would I ever dream of replacing my own mother in form or feature. I'm exceedingly grateful for her continuous support and wise guidance in my life. I love her. No one could ever take her place, but I praise God for providing me with the perfect fill-in in every stage of my life.

I thank God for the rare and beautiful collection of moms He has given me around the world. I've tucked them into my treasure chest of memories.

Prayer: *Lord, thank you for proving your love for me through your willing servants. Bless them richly today.*

Thought for the Day: Be open to the mentors God provides in your life.

39

ON THE ROAD AGAIN

René Taubensee

I am the vine; you are the branches.
—John 15:5

My marriage doesn't fit the usual mold. My husband, Eddie, and I spent the first three-and-a-half months of our marriage together day and night. Then came six weeks of high stress, followed by our first move. Just a few weeks later we moved a second time—across the country with only a half day's notice.

We moved about every six months. Well, I say *we*, but it was mostly me—I'm a major league baseball wife.

Our routine was different than that of most couples. I saw my husband from about 11 A.M. to 2 P.M. each day, and we had dinner together at 1 A.M.

I learned to pack a box quickly and pare everything down to the basics. We went through three years of this routine. Then we hit our first major obstacle: a baby! It wasn't that we weren't happy about the birth of our son. But Dad left the day after his birth on a ten-day business trip. We got through it quite well, actually.

Two years later we had another baby and then another baby two years after that. You might say we had a rhythm going.

Our kids grew accustomed to sleeping in a darkened room until 10:00 A.M. Then we played the "Don't-wake-Daddy-yet" game. We ate at strange hours. Cracker Barrel was our favorite restaurant, because they serve breakfast all day, and our days started late.

The kids and I routinely fly to three cities in nine days—without Dad. Flying allows us to spend more time with him. We have decided to see our lives as a big adventure. When word comes that we're moving again to another city, it's just part of the game. Our latest relocation made it 23 moves in 10 years.

Another part of the game is playing cards and reading books in a hospital waiting room while Dad has surgery—seven surgeries so far.

Most people think this life is glamorous. The truth is that it's a hard life of moving, being alone, responsibilities, and people we don't know who are familiar with every detail of our lives. Patience is the key.

To be sure, there are great benefits to life as a major league baseball family, as long as we don't get caught up in it and forget reality. Reality is that our lives can quickly turn into tough challenges: one day the fans love us; the next they can't stand us. One day we're all settled in; the next day we're off to another city.

How have we kept our heads out of the clouds? How do we keep our marriage and family strong when we spend so much time apart and in transition? How do we raise our kids when their roots grow only two inches deep?

We stay connected to the Vine! We abide—or rest—in Christ. In John 15:5 Jesus said, "I am the vine; you are the branches. If a man remains in me and I in him, he will bear much fruit; apart from me you can do nothing."

Early in our marriage we understood that apart from Jesus we could do nothing of eternal value. We dedicated our lives to our Lord and Savior Jesus Christ and decided to see life through His eyes and to view it as a great adventure. Everywhere we go, we surrounded ourselves with people who have taught us the Word of God. This has equipped us with knowledge about how to live our lives as ambassadors for Christ in a public spotlight.

God has taught us to rely fully on Him. We have learned to be secure in the knowledge that even though we may be caught off guard, worn down by circumstances, and ready to give up sometimes, He never is. His grace and guidance sustain us, keeping us humble in the great times and lifted up in the not-so-great times.

Still, in those early years I was a busy mom with three kids and a husband on the road. There were days when the only time I could spend with God was behind a locked bathroom door or praying in the shower. The great truth is that none of that matters to God. He's not concerned with the details of how we spend time with Him, just that we're constantly making that effort.

It doesn't matter who we're married to, where we live, or

how many kids we have. Mothers need to be refreshed and renewed by spending time with Him. Those precious moments are important to those of us raising children. They're key to being able to do what God has put before us.

We moms must be consistent in our dedication to Him, because our kids are watching us, and they'll learn to relate to Him through what they see in us. When we communicate with God through prayer and Bible study, we can teach our children the truth from God's Word in ways that encourage them to communicate their struggles and joys with Him as well.

By staying in close communion with the Lord, I've been able to roll with life's changes and challenges—even though our family's theme song is "On the Road Again."

Prayer: *Father, thank you so much for being with me wherever the path of life takes me.*

Thought for the Day: Staying attached to the Vine is the key to producing fruitful lives, rich and bursting with the flavor of Christ-likeness.

40 MY PRAYING MOTHER

Lai Sabrina Minh Tu

I prayed for this child, and the Lord has granted what I asked.
—I Sam. 1:27

The inky blackness of the starless sky was very frightening to me. Our tiny boat was tossed about in the turbulent, swelling sea just off the shore of Vietnam. My family of five was finally realizing a dream of escaping to freedom from our embattled country, Vietnam, on April 12, 1977. I was just eight years old, and although it was scary, it was also exciting to finally be underway.

There were 46 of us crowded into that little 12 x 20 craft. We had made plans to flee Communist oppression for many months. Finally, the escape was happening. We huddled closely together to keep warm, praying that the border patrols would not find us and thanking God for the covering of darkness. Our future was uncertain, but we were united in our urgent need to be free. We were eager to get to the refugee camp in Thailand.

Prior to the communist takeover, my mother, Nam, had been one of the wealthiest people in our city of Dalat. However, the Communists had taken almost everything of material value. Through my maternal grandparent's faith in God, my mother became a believer at a young age. So she held on to what had eternal value—her unwavering faith in God. Nobody could take that from her! Her prayers and strength in the Lord sustained our family throughout the years of oppression as we dreamed of liberation.

During the first few days, our tiny boat headed due northwest. The adults worked continuously, bailing water to remain afloat. Many suffered from seasickness and dehydration. I was unconscious for two days because of dehydration. Once again my mother prayed, and I regained consciousness. On the fourth day a Thai shrimp boat suddenly appeared. The burly, angry-looking fishermen forced us to a seemingly deserted island. But it was not deserted. Pirates inhabited the island, and they charged our boat, pulling out pistols and shotguns. They threatened the men and robbed us of everything of material value.

Our family thought we had escaped, but then a huge pirate roughly grabbed my three-year-old sister, Thuan. One objective of the pirates was to capture young girls to use for prostitution. Risking her own life, Mother courageously charged the pirate and pulled Thuan from his arms.

Miraculously, neither of them was killed. The pirates and fishermen left, and our tattered little group once again set sail, finally arriving in Thailand. We were near starvation, suffering from dehydration, sunburn, and the ravages of the attack. But Mother's strong faith remained intact along with our desire to be free.

After landing, we walked a long stretch of bumpy road to

the refugee camp, limping and stopping frequently to help the ones who were sick. However, our troubles were not over when we arrived at the camp. Because of our bedraggled appearance and incoherence from exhaustion, we were kept in isolation for several weeks and were treated as inferior, undesirable, and unstable aliens. Sadly, this treatment lasted throughout our eight months in the camp.

To survive, we fished or hunted every day, scratching out a meager living. We had no shelter and slept on the ground. We had very little contact with the outside world. It was easy to question whether this was really God's plan, but Mother continued to pray. As she talked about God's deliverance in the past, our faith was restored.

Finally, a letter came from an uncle in the United States. He made arrangements for us, and our little family arrived in Oklahoma City on April 12, 1978. Freedom at last!

The following years involved many moves, adjustments, new schools, a new language, and adapting to a totally different culture. Underlying everything was our mother's prayers and strong faith, along with her belief that God would continue to guide us.

One day, when I was 10, an American man kidnapped me on my way to school. As I kicked and screamed, I prayed as Mother had taught me. After carrying me many blocks, he finally dropped me onto the sidewalk, leaving me unharmed. Again, God answered prayer.

When I was 12 and we were living in Boston, we heard that a great evangelist, Billy Graham, was coming to town. Eagerly, my family and many of our friends went to the meetings. As they were singing "Just as I Am" one evening, I found myself joining the throngs of people streaming to the front. As I prayed with Rev. Graham, I gave my heart to the Lord. Again, my mother's prayers were answered.

I loved school and learned English rapidly. I graduated from high school with high honors and won scholarships to college. I planned to become an engineer. However, during my freshmen year at college, the Lord spoke to me very clearly, calling me into ordained ministry. I wrestled with this call, begging the Lord to allow me to pursue engineering so I could provide for my family. But God's plan became clearer and more intense. Finally, I surrendered, responding wholeheartedly to His call.

My family moved to Tampa, Florida. We became very involved in the Vietnamese ministry at a local church. Mother continued to pray for us. I shared God's call and my desire to serve in ministry with Frank, one of the sponsors. He told me a church in Clearwater, Florida, had begun a Vietnamese work and needed someone to lead it.

I met with the senior pastor, Mark Lancaster, and Joyce Williams, Minister of Outreach and Christian Education. As we shared together, the presence of the Lord was very real. As a result, I became pastor of that Vietnamese congregation. What a joy it was to minister to my people!

While serving at the church in Clearwater, my mother and I continued to pray for God's guidance and leading in my life. A couple of years later, God opened the door for me to pioneer a Vietnamese church in Tarpon Springs, Florida.

I also worked with World Relief Organization, helping to resettle many refugees. God opened many doors for me to share His love with them. During the first three years of the ministry, 85 people accepted the Lord Jesus Christ as personal Savior.

Seven years later, God opened the door for our congregation to relocate to Tampa and share the gospel with all people.

Throughout the years my mother has always prayed faithfully. Many days she is praying by 3 A.M. Once I stood by my mother's bedroom door and heard her simple prayer: *God, please help and strengthen Lai as she continues to fulfill your call in her life.* Her prayers have given me the strength and the courage to continue.

I thank God for answering Mother's prayers and sparing me from oppression, death, ravaging pirates, starvation, and kidnapping. The Lord enabled me to graduate from college with a bachelor of arts degree in pastoral ministries with a minor in missions; and a master of divinity from Asbury Theological Seminary.

But the most important lesson I have ever learned has been to follow Mother's example in prayer.

Prayer: *Father, thank you for mothers who pray. Help me be a faithful, praying mother.*

Thought for the Day: There's nothing more beautiful than a mother on her knees.

41

SUSANNAH WESLEY

Joyce Williams

She speaks with wisdom, and faithful instruction is on her tongue.
—Prov. 31:26

Susannah Wesley is recognized as a wonderful and effective mother. Her teachings and instructions are still highly revered today. All of us admire the incredible accomplishments of her children.

She was born in 1669, the youngest of 25 children. She loved to read and turned to the Bible to find the truth. Her father was a godly minister who refused to obey an English law of 1662 forcing all clergymen to obey *The Book of Common Prayer.* As a result, he suffered much persecution. During that time, 5,000 Christians called "nonconformists" died in English prisons for their faith.

Her father instilled within Susannah a strong desire to make her life count through Christian service. He told her that England needed someone to light a candle and hold it high so the people could find their way out of the spiritual darkness of that day. She wanted so much to help others to come to know Christ, and she prayed each day, *Dear God, make my life count.*

Susannah married Samuel Wesley, a minister who shared her determination to spread the truth—regardless of the consequences. They went through many difficult times and were persecuted because the truth was not fashionable. But they held tightly to their faith. Susannah worked hard nurturing her children's knowledge and faith in God, even under extremely difficult circumstances.

Susannah gave birth to 19 children. Ten of their children died before they were two years old, and one daughter was deformed. Yet Susannah wrote in her diary that all her suffering and loss served to "promote my spiritual and eternal good. Glory be to Thee, O Lord."

She came to realize the best way of serving God was to invest herself fully in instilling within all her children a great desire to change the world. She determined to raise these children dedicated to the Lord.

Samuel tried to remain with the Church of England. For this, his barns were burned and his own disgruntled congregation had him arrested and thrown into prison. During this time, Susannah endured terrible poverty. A thief slashed the udders of the family cow so she had to find milk for her family elsewhere. Yet her faith remained secure as she declared, "Religion is nothing else than doing the will of God and not our own."

She home-schooled her children six hours a day. One day the roof of their house was burned by irate parishioners. All the family escaped unharmed except for six-year-old John, who jumped from a window as the roof caved in. Thankfully, he suffered only minor injuries.

Susannah Wesley believed that for a child to grow into a self-disciplined adult, he or she must first be a parent-disciplined child. To her, the stubborn flesh was the hardest battle for Christians to fight, and godly parents would do well to equip their children to overcome it early. She expressed this succinctly.

When the will of a child is totally subdued, and it is brought to revere and stand in awe of the parents, then a great many childish follies . . . may be passed by. . . . I insist on the conquering of the will of children betimes, because this is the only strong and rational foundation of a religious education. . . . When this is thoroughly done, then a child is capable of being governed by reason and piety.

It was the courageous, tenacious faith of this Bible-believing woman that gave Christendom two of the most important figures of the eighteenth century. John grew up to become one of the greatest preachers and missionaries of all times. He founded the Methodist Church and was later barred from most of the churches in England, so he traveled to America to spread the gospel. Charles is remembered for hundreds of hymns that have brought joy and hope across the centuries.

She died on July 23, 1742, but in response to her father's challenge, the candles of faith Susannah Wesley ignited—along with her God-given wisdom—are still burning brightly today.

Prayer: *Heavenly Father, please enable me to ignite eternal flames of faith in the lives of my children.*

Thought for the Day: "When the will of a child is totally subdued, and it is brought to revere and stand in awe of the parents, then a great many childish follies may be passed by" (Susannah Wesley).

A TAMED TONGUE

Susan Vick

No man can tame the tongue.
—James 3:8

My smart mouth had gotten me into another mess. As a result, I was whisked off to a grandmother I didn't know and subsequently to a Bible camp. Ah, Bible camp as punishment—there's nothing better.

I was 13 and had what I considered to be a gifted tongue; Mom thought it was a curse. During my two-week camp internment I did beautifully, acting as if I didn't care and found the whole thing boring. Truthfully, late one night I quietly asked Jesus to forgive me and to be my Savior. I figured there was no reason to tell anybody. Jesus knew.

All I knew about Christianity at that point was that I was supposed to be out offending believers and nonbelievers alike by cramming my ideas down their throats. So I decided I was going to keep my salvation very quiet and learn about God without any help. I just needed to figure out how to pray. Did I say *God* or *Jesus*? Would God answer if I didn't mention *Mary*?

I didn't know. Did I need to close my eyes or open them? Should I kneel or sit when I prayed? Should I fold my hands a certain way?

I started out by praying for a few things I wanted such as boyfriends and clothes, and my prayers were answered. So God moved His way up to "Genie in the bottle" status. I was a happy Christian as long as Jesus granted my prayer requests. You may have guessed that my spiritual life was short-lived.

The Holy Spirit was working with me, but I was running. I started experimenting with drugs. Acid and speed were the new things. My mother and stepfather tried to intervene the best way they knew by forcing me to go to church. Ah, church for punishment—there's nothing better.

Late one night, a drug I took turned into a bad trip. For the first time in a long time I asked God for help. The next morning I made it official and let my best friend know that I was a Christian and would no longer be doing drugs.

To this day, I remember what she said: "Take a bottle of aspirin and call me in the morning." I was afraid of losing my friends, but when that happened, I wasn't as crushed as I thought I would be. God was about to supply me with mentors who would love me and challenge me.

It must have been the next Sunday that I went forward and made assurance of my salvation. Later I made a public profession of my faith by being baptized. I was no longer a secret Christian. I openly acknowledged that I was a former sinner who had been saved by grace. I quickly went to the task of offending believers and nonbelievers alike by cramming my ideas down their throats. If I had spent some time in the Scriptures, I would have had fewer people to apologize to.

It wasn't long before God placed Mary and Judy, sisters, in my life. They became my first mentors. They took me under their wings and began telling me how they had become Christians. We discovered that we had a lot in common. One of my most life-changing experiences was as they shared with me as we sat around a bonfire. We talked for hours. They taught me how to pray and showed me how to have a daily quiet time. They stood by me even when I was busy offending believers and nonbelievers alike. They patiently worked with me—God knew exactly what I needed.

God has continued to bless me with many other wonderful mentors. They have shared their very personal walks with me, and I continue to be blessed every day because of them. God used my mentors to teach me to listen first, pray second, and speak last.

I was privileged to witness to some of the people who had known me during my dark days. God saw to it that their paths crossed mine—some in unusual ways, ways that have shown me that our Lord has quite a sense of humor.

I must confess that guarding what I say remains a challenge for me, so I'm grateful that God is still in the tongue-taming business today.

Prayer: *Thank you, Father, for taming my tongue. Help me to think before I speak.*

Thought for the Day: Surrendered lives are filled with praise to the Lord.

43

BLENDED BLESSINGS

Jennifer Zollinger

"I know the plans I have for you," declares the LORD,
"plans to prosper you and not to harm you,
plans to give you hope and a future."
—Jer. 29:11

I expected my marriage to last. I never wanted to wear the scars of divorce, nor did I want that for my children. It was important to me to keep my commitments—even when it hurt. I was devastated the night I returned to our home in Mississippi after visiting family in Kansas. My husband had moved out, emptied the bank account, and left divorce papers on the dining room table.

It was the summer of 1994, and my life seemed to crumble around me. I knew the Lord hated divorce, and so did I. I was sure he would change my husband's heart, but after a three-year separation, the divorce became final.

I was ashamed to be a divorced person. I've heard it said, "When you feel like a throwaway person, you act like a throwaway person." For years I wore dark clothes and hoped

Blended Blessings

people wouldn't notice me, especially men. How could I ever trust another man?

I loved being a mom, however, and I put all my energy into raising my two children and being involved in their lives. I went to church but felt that I no longer belonged. My family lived close by, and they were a great encouragement to me. With them, I didn't feel as if I were a second-class citizen.

I didn't think of myself in that way with the Lord either. My daily devotion time was precious, and His Word spoke to my heart. One of my favorite passages during that time was Col. 3:12 in which we're reminded that we're chosen and dearly loved.

During that time I began to do all kinds of self-improvement things. I read, went to seminars, took classes, and discovered new interests. I enjoyed growing. Slowly I began healing and became more comfortable with who I was, including my status as a single mom. I joined a Sunday School class for single mothers and enjoyed developing friendships with other ladies in my situation.

The Lord seemed especially near during this time and provided for my family in amazing ways. I claimed Isa. 54:5: "Your Maker is your husband, the LORD Almighty is his name." That promise was kept over and over.

For many years after my divorce I had no interest in meeting men. But I slowly changed my mind and cautiously began to date. I got to know some really great men, but those relationships never felt quite right. I sensed the Lord's whisper in my heart: *Wait for my best.*

Finally He put a desire in my heart to remarry. My children shared this desire, and we began to pray for God's choice. I asked the Lord to be the author of my love story and to make it obvious when I met the right man. I knew if the Lord picked a husband for me, he would be wonderful. I even had the nerve to ask God to "knock my socks off" with His choice, claiming Heb. 4:16—"Let us then approach the throne of grace with confidence."

As we prayed, I began to feel the Lord revealing things about the man he was bringing. I knew he would have a broken heart and that it would become my calling to help restore the brokenness and lost relationships. I knew somehow that we would share an interest in health. This may sound strange, but I also believed his first name would begin with the letter J.

I met Joe in 2004 while working at Wichita State University. He was a guest speaker for one of our health and wellness programs. I immediately felt a connection with him, but the Lord had taught me to not think about a man as a potential date until I first knew he was a Christian and single.

With that quickly established, we began to spend time together and meet each other's friends and family. We found that we knew some of the same people, had attended the same concerts and seminars, and ate at the same restaurants. It was like we traveled in the same circles, not meeting until we were both ready.

Joe's parents and two youngest children welcomed me warmly and became great friends with my children. His three older children, though always kind, were more reserved. They had been mistreated by their stepmother and were wary of the new woman in their dad's life.

Our courtship was a wonderful answer to our prayers and a dream come true. Joe was everything the kids and I had prayed for. Eph. 3:10 was truly fulfilled in my life—"[He] is able to do immeasurably more than all we ask or imagine."

I was overwhelmed by God's love for me in bringing Joe into my life and knew our love was divinely designed. I was confident He had something special planned for us as a couple. After meeting with many leaders for wise counsel and sharing our story, we were unanimously given the blessing to marry.

Our life together has been very full. Over time, the older children have come to accept me. We try to stay involved in all our children's lives and be available to them when they need us. When we part there are hugs, and we warmly tell each other, "I love you."

One of the most special blessings that came out of joining our families is the precious relationship between my daughter and Joe's father. They had an affinity for each other from the beginning but have developed a special bond since the recent death of Joe's mother.

Joe and I work together at his chiropractic clinic and our Internet franchising business. Through all the busyness of family, friends, work, church, home, and pets, we try to connect each day and remind ourselves that we are God's gift to each other.

We feel strongly called by God to share hope with other blended couples and families. Combining families can present unique challenges, but the blessings can outweigh the struggles. We're currently involved in the process of starting a ministry to blended families at our church. Our calling is to share the firm belief that even after divorce, God can take the broken pieces of one's life and make something beautiful to be used for His glory.

And when God blends a family, the sweet mixture is a glorious treat.

Prayer: *Heavenly Father, thank you for taking fractured lives and making them into something new and joyous.*

Thought for the Day: God does His best work when we're in our deepest distress.

44

QUIET MOMENTS

Joyce Williams

Father, in your Word we read
That your Son often withdrew
To solitary places,
Where He spent time with you.

Those precious, intimate times,
Cherished by Father and Son
Are models we must follow
So life's battles may be won.

But I must confess it's hard
As a mom to be still and wait
When pressures of daily life
Seem overwhelmingly great.

That's when I find that I must
Take time to step out of the race,
To pause and to listen for
Your words of love, hope, and grace.

For it's in those quiet moments
Carved from life's frantic pace
That I hear your sweet, gentle whisper
That soothes my turbulent days.

You take this mother's worn hand
And massage my frantic heart,
Flooding me with joy and peace,
Giving me a fresh new start.

So today I seek your peace
In this quiet and sheltered place,
To wait and listen for you
To calm my day's hectic pace.

Then when storms rage all around
And floods threaten to break through,
I know that you will be with me,
'Cause I've spent time alone with you.

ABOUT THE CONTRIBUTORS

Gracia Burnham: Gracia and her late husband, Martin, served as missionaries in the Philippines for 17 years. They were kidnapped by militant terrorists and held captive for more than a year. Martin was killed during their rescue. Gracia is a gifted speaker and author. She and her children live in Rose Hill, Kansas.

Judy Horn Anderson: Judy is a former music teacher and a pianist and vocalist. Now a successful realtor, she speaks frequently, sharing her valley and mountaintop experiences. Judy and her husband, Daryl, live in Wichita, Kansas. Between them they have four living children.

Karen Anderson: Karen works closely with her husband, Mark, who is president of Global Pastors Network and the Billion Soul Campaign. Karen also partnered with him when he was a pastor and church planter in several nations. They have six children and live in Lee's Summit, Missouri.

Susan Meredith Beyer: Susan is a former television host and producer of Christian talk shows. She has also served with GSF Media, writing promotional materials and coordinating events for National Religious Broadcasters. She currently serves with the Nashville Connection for Women in Christian Media. She and her husband, Philip Paul Beyer, live with their six children near Nashville.

Donna Bond: Donna is a busy wife, mother, and teacher. She teaches remedial reading to children of military parents at Ft. Riley, Kansas. She is active in children's and women's ministries in the church her husband, Jim, pastors. They live in Junction City, Kansas, with their three sons.

Rhea Briscoe: Rhea is an active keynote and conference speaker who desires to help women experience the freedom and power found in Jesus Christ. She and her husband, David, have seven children. David and Rhea minister to others in their home, their church, and at conferences and retreats. They live in the Milwaukee area.

Gail Buchanan: Gail is an accomplished musician. She has sung with many groups, including the Singing Quakers. She and her husband have two children. They live in Andover, Kansas.

Angela Eby: Angela has a degree in biblical studies, is a writer, and is the mother of three. She and her husband, Joe, live with their children in Louisburg, Kansas.

Judi Eby: Judie is the mother of three grown sons. She enjoys her friends, her dogs, reading, and nurturing her sons and their families. She and her husband, Don, live in Overland Park, Kansas.

Sherrie Eldridge: Sherrie is an author and the founder and president of an adoption educational organization, Jewel Among Jewels Adoption Network, Inc. She has two grown daughters and is a grandmother. Sherrie and her husband, Bob, live in Fishers, Indiana.

Brenda Fowler: Brenda has traveled to many countries on 35 short-term missions trips. She ministers through Bible study and interactive women's ministries. She and her husband, Tom, live near their two sons and their families in the Blue Ridge Mountains of Virginia.

Cheri Fuller: Cheri is a speaker and the author of many books. She and her husband, Holmes, live in Edmund, Oklahoma. They have three grown children.

Kendra Graham: Kendra is a registered nurse. She is supportive of her husband, Wil, who is following in the footsteps of his father, Franklin, and grandfather Billy Graham in conducting crusades around the world. Kendra and Wil live with their three children in Swannanoa, North Carolina.

Liz Curtis Higgs: Liz is an internationally known speaker and the bestselling author of 25 books, including *Bad Girls of the Bible.* She and her husband, Bill, have two children and live in Louisville, Kentucky.

Aletha Hinthorn: Aletha is a writer and speaker. She is the author of numerous books and articles including *Satisfied Heart Topical Bible Study Series.* She is the founder of Women Alive Ministries and editor of *Come to the Fire* magazine. She and her husband, Dan, live in the Kansas City area.

Lyndell Hetrick Holtz: Lyndell is a speaker and the author of *Confessions of an Adulterous Christian Woman.* She and her husband, David, live in St. Louis and are the parents of four children.

Shirley Hostetler: Shirley is a registered nurse. She is a mother and grandmother and very active in her church. She lives in Hutchinson, Kansas.

Cynthia Spell Humbert: Cynthia is a speaker, writer, and Christian therapist. Formerly associated with Minirth-Meyer Clinic, she now works primarily with women helping them overcome issues that are rooted in shame. She and her husband, David, are the parents of three children and live in Austin, Texas.

Becky Hunter: Becky is the president of Global Pastors Wives Network and the author of *Being Good to Your Husband on Purpose.* She and her husband, Joel, a senior pastor, are the parents of three married sons and live in Orlando, Florida.

Sarah Johnson: Sarah, a busy wife and mother, attended Wichita State University. She and her husband, Dale, have five children. They live in Wichita, Kansas.

Linn Kane: Linn is a paramedic who devotes herself to helping others by counseling adults and juveniles who suffer from a wide range of behavioral difficulties. Linn currently resides in Bartlesville, Oklahoma.

Carol Kent: Carol is an author and speaker. She is the founder and president of Speak Up for Hope and Speak Up Speaker Services. She and her husband, Gene, have one son and live in Florida.

Vicki Lancaster: Vicki is a nursing student. She is active in her local church and enjoys working with teens. She lives in Olive Branch, Mississippi.

Cindy Lipscomb: Cindy is the former vice-president and general manager of a large department store in Memphis. She currently serves as chairman and executive producer of a nonprofit community theatre that she founded following the deaths of two of her daughters. Cindy and her husband Mat, live near Memphis with their daughter Jesse Anne.

Stephanie Dawn London: Stephanie is an artist specializing in wedding gown replicas. She enjoys sharing her testimony and her search for femininity with teens and other women. She travels to New York on various assignments and resides in Wichita, Kansas.

Gail MacDonald: Gail is a wife, mother, grandmother, author, speaker, and counselor. Gail teaches primarily on spiritual discipline, relationships, and leadership. She has ministered with her husband, Gordon, for more than 46 years. They live near their children and their children's families in Belmont, New Hampshire.

Sherri McCready: Sherri is an author and speaker. She and her husband, Shannon, a pastor, are ministering through a new church plant. Sherri and Shannon and their four children live in Asheville, North Carolina.

Jerene Marable: Jerene has served in numerous countries on short-term mission assignments. Jerene has one surviving daughter and lives in Conway, Arkansas.

Paula Martin: Paula is the office manager for a family-owned investment firm. She and her husband, Jerry, have two grown children and six grandchildren. They live in Andover, Kansas.

Regina Robinson: Regina is a pastor's wife, homemaker, worship leader, teacher, and speaker. A former professor at Liberty University, Regina and her husband, Jua, have two children, and live in Boston, where they have planted a church.

Cheryl Roland: Cheryl has directed and worked with district and national women's ministries in several areas of the country where she and David, her husband, have served. David and Cheryl have two daughters and live in Marion, Indiana.

Kim Singson: Kim assumed leadership responsibility in her denomination upon her husband's death. She and her late husband, T.S., authored two books in their native language: *The Happy Christian Family* and *Youth's Responsibility.* Kim currently oversees 38 churches in seven states of northeastern India. She has three children and a foster daughter. Kim lives with her family in Manipur, India.

Kathryn Sipper: Kathryn shares the transforming power and grace of God through her writing, media projects, and public speaking. Her husband, DuWayne, is founder and executive director of The Path of Citrus County, Florida, a homeless shelter that presents the gospel and a life-skills program to those in need. Kathryn is the development director of the shelter. They live in Citrus Springs, Florida.

QUIET MOMENTS

Hope Tallent: Hope has worked and volunteered in South Korea and Kenya. She currently works in World Missions at International Church of the Nazarene Headquarters. She lives in Kansas City..

René Taubensee: René serves as the Pro Athletes Outreach Ambassador to Major League Baseball. She and her husband, Eddie, an 11-year veteran of major league baseball, work together ministering to players and their wives. They have three sons and live in Issaquah, Washington.

Lai Sabrina Minh Tu: Lai is the pastor of two churches in Tampa, Florida. She is a speaker and writer who responded to God's call on her life to full-time Christian ministry at a young age. She lives in Tampa, Florida.

Susan Vick: Susan and her husband, Steven, build and manage assisted living facilities for the elderly. When they are not traveling, they are at home in Dallas. They have two children.

Joyce Williams: Joyce is the author of seven books, including *She Can't Even Play the Piano* and *Quiet Moments for Ministry Wives,* published by Beacon Hill Press of Kansas City. Joyce and her husband, Gene, are directors of Shepherds' Fold Ministries, which they founded to encourage and affirm pastors and their families. Joyce and Gene speak in many settings in the U.S. and internationally and have worked with ministries including numerous assignments with the Billy Graham Evangelistic Association. They live in Wichita, Kansas.

Jennifer Zollinger: Jennifer and her husband, Joe, are involved in a ministry that mentors nontraditional families. Joe is a chiropractor, and Jennifer has a master's degree in exercise science. They work together in their health-related business. They live in Wichita, Kansas, and are the parents of seven children.

"Each of these devotional nuggets, written by or about mothers from around the world, provides an oasis for weary moms. As you take a few minutes to drink deeply and draw strength from these words of wisdom, your soul will be refreshed and your heart warmed."

—GENEVA VOLLRATH,
president and CEO, Stonecroft Ministries

As a mother, finding time each day
to refresh and renew your relationship
with God can be challenging.

This engaging collection of meditations and stories is designed to help you spend a few moments with God wherever your day may take you. These short devotionals provide encouragement from moms who thoughtfully share experiences and insights that have helped them face the challenges of motherhood. Their inspiring, honest reflections of faith will help you focus on the strength and power of God and find rest in the loving comfort of His arms.

CONTRIBUTORS:

Judy Horn Anderson • Karen Anderson • Susan Meredith Beyer • Donna Bond • Rhea Briscoe • Gail Buchanan • Gracia Burnham • Angela Eby • Judie Eby • Sherrie Eldridge • Brenda Fowler • Cheri Fuller • Kendra Graham • Liz Curtis Higgs • Aletha Hinthorn • Lyndell Hetrick Holtz • Shirley Hostetler • Cynthia Spell Humbert • Becky Hunter • Sarah Johnson • Linn Kane • Carol Kent • Vicki Lancaster • Cindy Lipscomb • Stephanie Dawn London • Gail MacDonald • Sherri McCready • Jerene Marable • Paula Martin • Regina Robinson • Cheryl Roland • Kim Singson • Kathryn Sipper • Hope Tallent • Rene Taubensee • Lai Sabrina Minh Tu • Susan Vick • Jennifer Zollinger

JOYCE WILLIAMS is a native of Roanoke, Virginia. She is the author of seven books including *My Faith Still Holds* and *Quiet Moments for Ministry Wives* and has written articles for more than 30 magazines. She and her husband, Gene, are directors of Shepherds' Fold Ministries, which they founded to encourage and affirm pastors and their families. Joyce and Gene speak around the world and work with many ministries including assignments with the Billy Graham Evangelistic Association. They live in Wichita, Kansas.

RELIGION / CHRISTIAN LIFE / WOMEN

BEACON HILL PRESS
OF KANSAS CITY

Cover Design: DARLENE FILLEY
Cover Photography: DON PLUFF

ISBN 978-0-8341-2355-7

90000

9 780834 123557